Dave Barry's Guide to
MARRIAGE
AND/OR SEX

By Dave Barry

Illustrated by
Jerry O'Brien

Rodale Press, Emmaus, Pennsylvania

Printed in the United States of America on recycled paper containing a high percentage of de-inked fiber.

Library of Congress Cataloging-in-Publication Data

Barry, Dave.
    [Guide to marriage and/or sex]
    Dave Barry's guide to marriage and/or sex / by Dave Barry; illustrated by Jerry O'Brien.
        p.   cm.
    Includes index.
    ISBN 0–87857–725–4 (pbk.)
    1. Mate selection.   2. Dating (Social customs) 3. Marriage. I. Title.
II. Title: Guide to marriage and/or sex.
HQ801.B34   1987
646.7′7—dc19   87–18461
                              CIP

2 4 6 8 10 9 7 5 3 1   paperback

Contents

MAKE SURE YOUR MARRIAGE PROPOSAL IS DONE WITH CREATIVITY

HOWEVER, MAKE SURE THAT YOU KNOW YOUR SWEETHEART REAL GOOD

Introduction

Marriage is a wonderful thing. Everybody should get married unless he or she has a good reason not to, such as that he or she is the Pope. I personally have been married two times that I know of, and you don't hear me complaining.

What's the secret of a happy marriage? Call me a romantic if you want, but for me, the answer is the same simple, beautiful idea that has been making relationships work for thousands of years: separate bathrooms. You give two people room to spread out their toiletry articles, and you have the basis of a long-term relationship. But you make them perform their personal hygiene activities in the same small enclosed space, year in and year out, constantly finding the other person's bodily hairs stuck on their deodorant sticks, and I don't care how loving they were when they started out. I don't care if they were Ozzie and Harriet. They'll be slipping strychnine into each other's non-dairy creamer.

Of course even an ideal marriage, even a marriage where the bathrooms are 75 feet apart, is going to have a certain amount of conflict. This is because marriages generally involve males and females, which are not called "opposite sexes" for nothing.

Why Men and Women Have Trouble Getting Along

At the risk of generalizing, I would say that the basic problem can be summarized as follows:

WHAT WOMEN WANT: To be loved, to be listened to, to be desired, to be respected, to be needed, to be trusted, and sometimes, just to be held.

WHAT MEN WANT: Tickets for the World Series.

So we can see that men and women do not have exactly the same objectives in mind. Which is why, as a rule, the only time you see two people of the opposite sex who have achieved true long-term stability in a marriage is when at least one of them is in a coma.

This is strange, when you think about it. I mean, look around at the other species. Most of them are much stupider than humans are, not counting humans who pay to watch automobile races, yet they have their male-female relationships all worked out. Take squids. Squids may have tiny little brains, but they know exactly how to have relationships. The female squid goes into heat at exactly the right time, and all the male squids come around and wave their tentacles in exactly the most attractive way, and she picks out the one with the biggest suckers, or whatever and they mate. And they know exactly *how* to mate, the same way that squids have been mating for 46 million years, without any kind of formal instruction whatsoever.

Wouldn't that be great? I don't mean having sex with a squid. I don't recommend that unless you get truly desperate (see "The Singles Scene," in Chapter 1). I mean having everything all worked out between the sexes; having a *procedure*, where everybody knew what to do and what to expect, and nobody ever felt guilty or inadequate.

Yet here *we* are, humans, the most sophisticated species on Earth, having evolved over the course of millions of years to the point where many of us have satellite dishes on our lawns, and we have less savvy, in terms of our relationships, than invertebrates.

People say: "Well, if you want a marriage to succeed, you have to work at it." And I say: *Why?* It isn't fair! The other species don't have to work at it! They don't even have to *think* about it! Can you imagine a female snake agoniz-

TRUE LOVE

ing about why a male snake never pays attention to her? Or a male cockroach nervously asking a female, after sex, if it was Good for her? Of course you can't! Cockroaches can't talk! But you know what I mean. I mean we have a problem here.

To date, the efforts to solve this problem have consisted mainly of articles in women's magazines, the ones that always have the following general lineup of articles:

21 Fun Drapery Possibilities
5 Common Mascara Blunders
10 Quick and Easy
    Mayonnaise-Based Entrees
14 Ways to Tell If Your Child
    Is Shooting Up
11 Exciting Pudding Concepts
6 New and Extremely Dense
    Chocolate Desserts
147 Weight-Loss Ideas

Somewhere in there they always have an article with a title like "12 Tips for Getting Some Quantity of Romance Back into Your Marriage," featuring advice such as: "TIP NUMBER THREE: Try not to blow your nose during sex."

These articles are fine, except for one thing: Men don't read them. Men read the sports section, or action adventure novels where the main characters are males who relate to each other primarily via automatic weapons. True, sometimes there are women in these novels, but only for the purpose of having firm breasts.

Clearly what is needed is some kind of book that women *and* men would want to read, a book that could bring the sexes together and help them reach some common ground by means of a straightforward, common-sense discussion of all aspects of finding the right mate, falling in love with this person, getting married, and living happily ever after. This was exactly my goal, when I set out to write this book. Unfortunately, as you'll see, I failed completely, but what the hell—you already bought the book, so you might as well read it.

A Thoughtful Word of Advice Before You Get Started

You cannot have a successful relationship just by reading this book. For a relationship to succeed, both parties must be willing to work. Work, work, work, that's the key. Endless, constant, extremely difficult, unpaid work. More work than is involved in the construction of major bridges and tunnels. I am getting very tired just thinking about it.

Also there will be hard times along the way. Awful times. Terrible, horrible times. That is why this book includes helpful advice such as in Chapter 3, where we talk about adding zip to your sex life via Saran Wrap and other common household products, and also how to recognize the warning signs that your spouse is having an affair, and what kind of gun you should buy.

But we're getting ahead of ourselves. First you have to meet somebody.

CHAPTER 1

How to Find Somebody to Go on Dates with and Eventually Get Married to Who Is Not a Total Jerk

In getting into the field of marriage, one very important decision you must make is who, exactly, will be your spouse. I am not saying this is the *most* important decision. It is certainly not as important as selecting the right wedding caterer (see Chapter 6, "How to Have a Perfect Wedding No Matter What"). But

you should definitely give it some thought.

To know where to look for a marriage partner, you need to know what kind of person you want. For example, if you want to meet a person who likes to bowl, you would go to a bowling alley; whereas if you want to meet a person who is rich, sensitive, attractive, and intelligent, you would not. So your first step is to scientifically develop a "psychological profile" of your Ideal Mate.

How to Develop A Psychological Profile of Your Ideal Mate

Choose the phrase that you feel best completes the sentences below:

Wealth

The person I wish to have for a mate should be able to afford:

1. Scotland.
2. Occasional dinners out.
3. Underwear.

Sensitivity

The person I wish to have for a mate should be sensitive enough to:

1. Instantly be aware of my every mood.
2. Swerve to avoid driving over pedestrians.
3. Not deliberately back up and run over pedestrians a second time.

Personal Appearance

The person I wish to have for a mate should be attractive enough to:

1. Be a movie star.
2. Be a movie star's accountant.
3. Be a movie star's accountant's intestinal parasite.

Intelligence

The person I wish to have for a mate should be smart enough to:

1. Discuss great works of literature.
2. Hold great works of literature right side up.
3. Differentiate between great works of literature and food.

HOW TO SCORE: Add up the numbers corresponding to your answers, then check the chart below.

IF YOUR ANSWERS TOTAL . . .	YOU'RE MOST LIKELY TO FIND YOUR IDEAL MATE . . .
1 through 8	Married to somebody else.
9 through 15	Engaged to somebody else.
16	In prison.

Okay! Now that you have a good idea of what you're looking for, it's time to get out and join . . .

The Singles Scene

The Singles Scene is located in bars that are so dark and loud it's impossible to see or hear anybody else. You can meet, fall in love, and get engaged without ever getting a clear view of the other person, which can lead to a situation where you arrive at your wedding, with all your friends and relatives, and you discover that you are betrothed to a cigarette machine. (Which actually may not seem like such a total disaster, once you find out what else is available on the Singles Scene.)

To avoid this kind of embarrassment, you should do what other smart singles do: Before you sit down, go around the room discreetly shining a police flashlight into the other singles' faces. Once you have selected a likely looking one, you should sit down near this person and get into a spontaneous conversation.

How to Get into
A Spontaneous Conversation

In the old days, the way people got into conversations was the woman would take a cigarette out of her purse and pretend to look for a match, which was the signal for six or seven available lurking men to lunge toward her, Zippos flaming, sometimes causing severe burns.

Smoking, however, has pretty much lost its glamor, to the point where trying to get a strange male to light your cigarette in public would be viewed as comparable to trying to get him to pick your nose. Which is a shame, really, because men are deprived of the chance to feel bold and masculine and necessary in the hostile bar environment. It would be nice if we had a modern bar-meeting ritual. Like maybe the woman could come in with a jar of relish, and she could sit there pretending she couldn't get the lid off, and the man could come along and offer to help, and soon they would be engrossed in a fascinating conversation. ("Are you fond of relish? Huh! I am fond of relish myself!")

But for now, we are stuck with the system where one party has to boldly walk right up to the other party and, with no real excuse, attempt to start a conversation. At one time this was strictly the man's responsibility, but now, what with Women's Liberation, it is still strictly the man's responsibility.

Men, this is nothing to be nervous about. After all, why do you think the woman came to a singles bar, if not to

KNOW YOUR SINGLES BARS !

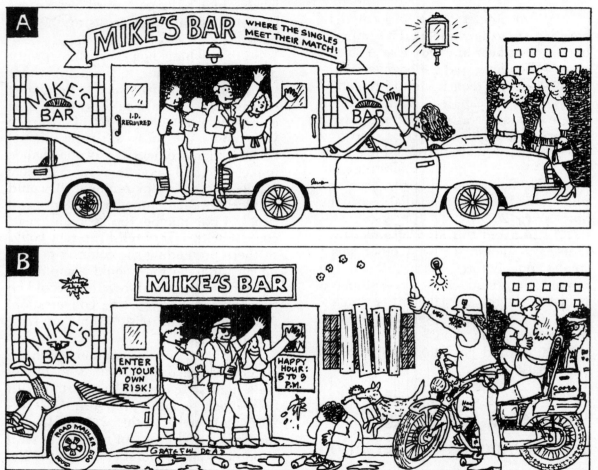

WHICH DIMLY LIT, CROWDED SINGLES BAR WOULD BE YOUR BEST BET TO FIND A DATE IN?

ANSWER: BAR "A" IS YOUR BEST BET, UNLESS YOU ALREADY HAVE A VENEREAL DISEASE

WHAT YOU HOPE TO FIND IN A SINGLES BAR

GREAT LOOKING GUYS

GREAT LOOKING GIRLS

WHAT IS ACTUALLY AVAILABLE

meet a guy like you, only smarter and more attractive? So go to it!

The trick is to know some good "opening lines" that are guaranteed to get a woman's attention and make her realize you are a caring and sharing kind of guy who has things on his mind such as international politics and great literature, and who doesn't just want to grope her body.

Some Good Opening Lines

- "How about those problems in the Middle East?"
- "How about those Brothers Karamazov?"
- "I don't just want to grope your body. I mean, not here in the bar."

What the Woman Should Do If She Is Not Interested

She should attempt to fend the male off via one of the following gently tactful yet firm statements:

- "Haha HA HA HA (cough cough cough) (spit)."
- "I'm sorry, but I just washed my hair."
- "I'm sorry, but unfortunately you hold no more physical attraction for

me than those photographs you sometimes see of a cold virus magnified several million times."

If subtlety doesn't work, if the man turns out to be the type who views himself as such an extreme Stud Muffin that he cannot imagine a woman who would not want to conceive a child via him, then the woman should take a more direct approach, such as Mace.

Meeting People through Personal Ads

These are those little paid advertisements that people take out in magazines or newspapers. A lot of people laugh at these ads, but in fact this is the way top stars such as Johnny Carson and Joan Collins get most of their spouses.

If you want your ad to be effective, however, it must have certain characteristics:

1. *It should say you are profoundly attractive.* Nobody in the personal ads, nobody, is ever "average-looking." If, for example, you had Elephant Man's Disease, you would describe yourself as "rugged."

2. *It should be extremely specific.* For example, if you're a man, you don't just say you're looking for "a nice

SWM — RUGGED NON-SMOKER, NON-DRINKER, NON-SWEARER, 30-YEAR-OLD CHRISTIAN WITH A WONDERFUL SENSE OF HUMOR SEEKS A SWF, SBF, SHF, OR SINGLE FEMALE OF ANY RACE OR SPECIES FOR LOVE, COMPANIONSHIP, AND ROMANTIC STROLLS IN THE MOONLIGHT ALONG THE BEACH. ALSO MUST ENJOY THE FINER THINGS IN LIFE: BOWLING, GOLF, POLKAS, BINGO, AND LOTS OF RAW UNINHIBITED SEX. NO ACCOUNTANTS OR TEXANS, PLEASE.
RESPOND TO NO. 147A

147A

woman." You say you're looking for "a 5'8" 23-year-old blonde Capricorn woman of Croatian ancestry weighing 109 pounds and having a degree in cultural anthropology from Duke University." This lets everybody know you are in a position to pick and choose, and not some semi-desperate schlump who has to advertise for dates.

SWF — CUTE, CUDDLY, AND THOROUGHLY LOVEABLE, HARDWORKING, COURTEOUS HOMEBODY SEEKS ANY MAN WHO ENJOYS WALKING ALONG THE BEACH, GOOD FOOD, GOOD MUSIC, AND LOTS OF CONVERSATION. AGE IS NO BARRIER AS LONG AS YOU ARE ALIVE. IF YOU WANT A FIRST-CLASS COOK WHO KNOWS HER WAY AROUND _EVERY_ ROOM IN THE HOUSE, I'M YOUR LADY! NO SMOKERS, DRINKERS, OR PERVERTS PLEASE. NO UGLY MEN NEED RESPOND.
RESPOND TO NO. 173C

173C

3. _It should say you like "candle-light dinners and long walks on the beach."_ All personal classified ads contain this phrase, not because anybody really _wants_ to take long walks on the beach, but because people want to prove they're Romantic and Sensitive. The beaches of America are teeming with couples who met because of personal ads, staggering along, sweating, and picking sea-urchin spines out of their feet, each person afraid to reveal to the other that he or she would rather be watching a rental movie.

Meeting People through Clubs and Organizations

Often it seems that the happiest marriages are the ones where the man and the woman share an interest in a hobby, like bass fishing. Because of this shared interest, such couples can pass countless intimate hours together, talking bait, plus they can use their vacation time to go on long fishing trips to secluded wilderness areas where they will find time to just be alone together, hour after hour, day after day, on some scum-encrusted, mosquito-infested lake, totally

FISHIN'

alone, until finally one of them disembowels the other with a scaling knife.

To get into a relationship like this, you need to develop an interest, preferably one that does not involve sharp implements, and go hang out with other people who have the same interest. Let's say, for example, that you have an interest in cats. Now I, personally, cannot imagine having any interest in cats other than to find out what happens when you submerge them for various lengths of time in roofing cement, but I am sure there are lots of formal pro-cat organizations in your area, which you could locate by asking a police officer. Go to their meetings and survey the crowd until you find a likely prospect to strike up a conversation with ("Hi! I see we share an interest in cats! Perhaps we should get married!").

If this doesn't work, you might try stamp collectors, or one of your major churches.

Meeting People at the Office

If you get an office job, you'll be involved in a serious relationship within a matter of days. This is the good news. The bad news is, this relationship will probably involve a person who is technically already married to somebody else. This is because, to a married person, the office is a highly romantic environment, where everybody wears nice clothes and discusses important issues such as the Three-Month Sales Forecast, in stark contrast to the home environment, where people tend to wear bathrobes with jelly stains on them and get into vicious day-long arguments over who put the ice tray back in the refrigerator with a dead roach in it (see Chapter 8, "How to Argue Like a Veteran Married Couple"). So the office becomes essentially a large, carpeted pit of illicit passion, where at least two-thirds of the activity is related to motel arrangements.

Whatever method you use to meet somebody, your next step is to go on a number (174) of dates so you can get to know what this person is really like.

Tips for Gals: 13 Common First-Date Warning Signs That a Guy Might Be a Jerk

1. He brings his mom.
2. He smells bad.
3. He smells a little too good.
4. He proudly carries the American Express Platinum Card.
5. He periodically blows his nose elaborately into a handkerchief, then folds it up carefully and puts it back into his pocket as though it was some kind of valuable artifact.
6. He wants to take you to a hockey game.
7. He wants to know if you know how to clean fish.
8. He always calls the waitress "Sweets."
9. He manages to let you know how much money he makes by some contrivance such as pulling a piece of paper out of his pocket and saying: "I'll be darned! Here's my W-2 form!"
10. He wears wing-tip shoes when he doesn't have to.
11. He has pictures of his car.
12. He has a personalized license plate on his car.
13. He has motivational cassette tapes in his car.

Dating

"Dating" simply means "going out with a potential mate and doing a lot of fun things that the two of you will never do again if you actually get married." Dating is a very important part of the mate-selection process throughout all of nature. Some sectors of nature, such as insects, date for only a few seconds; birds, on the other hand, perform an elaborate Dating Dance. In fact, dancing is all that

WHICH GUY IS THE JERK? WHICH GUY IS THE ACCOUNTANT? WHICH GUY IS THE MILLIONAIRE?

ANSWER: MR B IS ALL THREE: A MILLIONAIRE ACCOUNTANT JERK. THE OTHER THREE ARE SLIME.

birds *can* do, because in order to make it possible for them to fly, they cannot have sexual organs, which is why we have to import flocks of new birds from Canada every year.

Human beings dated as far back as ancient times, as is shown by the biblical quotation: "And Balzubio DID taketh Parasheeba to a restaurant, and they DID eateth potato skins." The next recorded date was between Romeo and Juliet, a young Italian couple who went out despite their parents' objections, and just about everybody involved ended up either stabbed or poisoned.

After this tragedy, there was very little dating for several centuries. During this time, marriages were arranged by the parents, based on such things as how much cattle the bride and the groom would each bring to the union. Often the young couple wouldn't even *meet* until the wedding, and sometimes they were not strongly attracted to each other. Sometimes, quite frankly, they preferred the cattle. So now we feel that dating is probably a better system.

Who Should Ask Whom for the Date

As we noted earlier, these are free and liberated and nonstereotypical times we live in, by which I mean it is the responsibility of the man to ask for the date, and the responsibility of the woman to think up excuses that get progressively more obvious until the man figures out that the woman would rather chew on a rat pancreas.

FAMOUS COUPLES THROUGHOUT HISTORY

THE WIZARD OF OZ AND DOROTHY

SAMSON AND DELILAH

TARZAN AND CHEETAH

ROMEO AND JULIET

Four Fun Things to Do on a Date

1. Go to a restaurant and have something to eat.

2. Go to a restaurant and have a completely different thing to eat.

3. Go to a completely different restaurant.

4. Go to visit interesting places such as New York and Europe and see if they have any restaurants.

Things You Can Talk About on a Date

1. Your various entrees.

Falling in Love

When two people have been on enough dates, they generally fall in love. You can tell you're in love by the way you feel: your head becomes light, your heart leaps within you, you feel like you're walking on air, and the whole world seems like a wonderful and happy place. Unfortunately these are also the four warning signs of colon disease, so it's always a good idea to check with your doctor.

But if it turns out to be love, it's time to think about taking the next major step in a relationship: French-kissing.

Ha ha! Just kidding. The next major step is to live in Sin, which we will

THE WORLD RECORD FOR MOST DATES IN ONE YEAR IS HELD BY NORMA LEE JOHNSON OF LAS VEGAS, NEVADA. IN 1986 SHE DATED 7,413 MEN.

cover in the next chapter. Of course if you belong to a religious sect that believes that a couple should get married first, you should skip the next chapter and go straight to the one about sex, unless it is a very strict religious sect, in which case you should burn this book immediately.

CHAPTER 2

Living in Sin

For many years, it was generally considered to be wrong to live in Sin. Now, however, thanks to the Sexual Revolution (May 6, 1967), living together is considered a normal and in fact very useful phase in a relationship, a phase that is accepted and even endorsed by virtually all sectors of society except of course your parents. Your parents hate it. It doesn't matter how nice or respectable the person is you're living with. You could be living with Abraham Lincoln, and your parents would still hate it. Especially if you are a guy.

But, hey, it's your life to live, and if you really want to move in with somebody, your feelings have to take precedence over your parents'. The best thing to do is confront their concerns head-on, by sitting down with them, face to face, and lying.

"Mom and Dad," you should say,

"Bill and I are *not* living together. He came over to my apartment this morning to help me kill a spider and by mistake he left his toothbrush and all his clothes and furniture."

Your parents will pretend they believe you, because the truth is they really don't want to even think about the idea of you and S-E-X. All parents are like this. No matter how old you get, in their minds you will always have the wisdom and emotional maturity of Beaver Cleaver.

Moving in Together

Moving in together is an exciting and romantic adventure for both of you, a time of caring and sharing the joys of little discoveries such as what another person's used dental floss looks like. But this is also a time when you must try to be practical. You must bear in mind that no matter how much you love each other now, somewhere down the road you will inevitably have traditional "lovers' quarrels" wherein one of you will hurl all of the other one's possessions out the window and possibly kill an innocent pedestrian. This is why most experts recommend that you get a ground-floor apartment furnished mainly with lightweight, easy-to-hurl Tupperware.

The Most Serious Issue Likely to Come between a Man and a Woman Living Together

(WARNING: Those of you who detest blatant and unfair but nonetheless generally true sexual stereotypes should leave the room at this time.)

Okay. The major issue facing a man and a woman who decide to live together is: Dirt. I am serious. Men and women do not feel the same way about dirt at all. Men and women don't even *see* dirt the same way. Women, for some hormonal reason, can see individual dirt molecules, whereas men tend not to notice them until they join together into clumps large enough to support commercial agriculture. There are exceptions, but over 85 percent of all males are legally classifiable as Cleaning Impaired.

This can lead to serious problems in a relationship. Let's say a couple has decided to divide up the housework absolutely even-steven. Now when it's the woman's turn to clean, say, the bathroom, she will go in there and actually clean it. The man, on the other hand, when it's his turn, will look around, and, because he is incapable of seeing the dirt, will figure nothing major is called for, so

LIVING TOGETHER DEMANDS SOME PREPLANNING

he'll maybe flush the toilet and let it go at that. Then the woman will say: "Why didn't you clean the bathroom? It's *fil-thy!*" And the man, whose concept of "filthy" comes from the men's rooms in bars, where you frequently see bacteria the size of cocker spaniels frisking around, will have no idea what she's talking about.

So what happens in most relationships is, the man learns to go through the motions of cleaning. Ask him to clean a room, and he'll squirt Windex around seemingly at random, then run the vacuum cleaner over the carpet, totally oblivious to the question of whether or not it's picking up any dirt.

I have a writer friend, Clint Collins, who once proposed that, as a quick "touch-up" measure, you could cut a piece of two-by-four the same width as the vacuum cleaner and drag it across the carpet to produce those little parallel tracks, which as far as Clint could tell were the major result of vacuuming. (Clint was also unaware for the first 10 or 15 years of his marriage that vacuum cleaners had little bags in them; he speculated that the dirt went through the electrical cord and into the wall.)

What this means is that, if your live-together relationship is going to work, both of you must be sensitive to the special needs of the Cleaning Impaired. Unfortunately for you women, this means you must spend many hours patiently going over basic cleaning concepts that may seem simple and obvious to you, but will be baffling mysteries to the Cleaning Impaired person, such as:

1. Where clean dishes actually come from.

2. What you can do with used pizza boxes besides stack them in the corner of the living room for upwards of two years.

3. How some people do more in the way of cleaning the bedroom than simply spray a few blasts of Right Guard deodorant on the two-foot-high mound of unlaundered jockey shorts.

And so on. The best way to avoid conflict is if you make up lists that state clearly what cleaning chores each of you will be responsible for. At first, the Cleaning Impaired person's list should be fairly modest:

NORMAL PERSON'S WEEKLY CHORE LIST	CLEANING IMPAIRED PERSON'S WEEKLY CHORE LIST
1. Clean kitchen. 2. Clean bathroom. 3. Clean entire rest of domicile.	1. Don't get peanut butter on sheets.

Speaking of peanut butter, another area where a first-time live-together couple can run into trouble is the kitchen. Here again we need to confront the depressing fact that, despite all the progress that has been made in other areas, such as coeducational softball, when it comes to sharing equally in food-preparation responsibilities, many men are still basically scumballs. I know I am. This was driven home to me on a recent Thanksgiving day, when my family had dinner at the home of friends named Arlene and Gene.

Picture a typical Thanksgiving scene: on the floor, three small children and a dog who long ago had her brain eaten by fleas are running as fast as they can directly into things, trying to injure themselves. On the television, the Detroit Lions are doing pretty much the same thing. In the kitchen, Arlene, a prosecuting attorney responsible for a large staff, is doing something to a turkey. Surrounding Arlene are thousands of steaming cooking containers. I would no more enter that kitchen than I would attempt to park a nuclear aircraft carrier, but my wife, who runs her own business, glides in very casually and picks up exactly the right kitchen implement and starts doing exactly the right thing without receiving any instructions whatsoever. She quickly becomes enshrouded in steam.

So Gene and I, feeling guilty, finally bumble over and ask what we can do to help, and from behind the steam comes Arlene's patient voice asking us to please keep an eye on the children. Which we try to do. But there is a famous law of physics that goes, "You cannot watch small children and the Detroit Lions at the same time, and let's face it, the Detroit Lions are more interesting." So we would start out watching the children, and then one of us would sneak a peek at the TV and say, "Hey! Look at this tackle!" And then we'd have to watch the Instant Replay to find out whether the tackled person was dead or just permanently disabled. By then the children would have succeeded in injuring themselves or the dog, and this voice from behind the kitchen steam would call, very patiently, "Gene, *please* watch the children."

I realize this is awful. I realize this sounds just like Ozzie and Harriet. I also realize that there are some males out there, with hyphenated last names, who have evolved much further than Gene and I have, who are not afraid to stay home full-time and get coated with baby vomit while their wives work as test pilots, and who go into the kitchen on a daily basis to prepare food for other people, as opposed to going in there primarily for beer. But I think Gene and I are more typical. I think most males rarely prepare food for others, and when

GENE AND DAVE WATCH TRANSFIXED WHILE FIDO DANCES FOR THE KIDS

they do, they have their one specialty dish (spaghetti, in my case) that they prepare maybe twice a year in a very elaborate production number, for which they expect to be praised as if they had developed, right there in the kitchen, a cure for heart disease.

What Men Have to Do about This

It's very simple, men. If you want to have a decent and fair live-together relationship, you have to start cooking whole entire meals all by yourself on a regular basis. And by "meals," men, I do not mean "Kraft Cheez Whiz eaten directly from the jar with a spoon." I mean meals that somebody *else* would eat. That even your *mom* would eat.

This is not as hard as you think, men. All you need to do is learn some "recipes."

Recipes for Guys

Recipe Number One: Food Heated Up

This dish has long been a specialty of women and the great chefs of Europe, who have learned that, with a few exceptions, such as grape soda, almost all food tastes better when you heat it up. In fact some foods, such as baked potatoes, are very hard to eat any other way.

TO PREPARE: Get enough units of food to feed yourself and the person you are living with. Now select a pot that you feel is the correct size. Now put this pot back and select another one, because the one you selected first was wrong. (Trust me here, guys. In 15 years, I have never once selected an initial pot that my wife did not feel, based on her vastly superior experience and hormonal instinct, was the wrong size.)

Okay. Now try to put the food unit inside the pot. (CULINARY HINT: For extra elegance, try removing the food unit from its can or wrapper first!) If it fits, cook it on top of the stove on "medium" heat until just before it overflows the top and wrecks the stove. If it doesn't fit into the pot, it's probably a turkey, a roast, or a ham, which you can tell by counting the number of legs and referring to this convenient chart:

FOOD TYPE	NUMBER OF LEGS	COOKING TEMPERATURE
Turkey	2	medium
Roast	0	medium
Ham	0	medium

These larger foods should be placed inside the little room under the stove (the "oven") and cooked on "medium" heat until just before they fill the entire dwelling area with dense acrid smoke.

IMPORTANT NOTE: If the food unit is, in fact, a turkey, be sure to check inside and remove the traditional Surprise Packet of yuckola blobs that is always found in the interiors of deceased frozen turkeys for reasons that nobody can really explain. One theory is that it is placed there as a protest by dissatisfied workers at the turkey manufacturing plant. A more plausible theory is that the blobs are actually dormant baby turkeys. Most savvy chefs immediately throw them into the garbage or flush them down the toilet, which incidentally is how there came to be giant albino turkeys in the New York City sewer system whose only natural enemies are the alligators.

Recipe Number Two: Two Kinds of Food in the Same Meal

Yes! This really is possible! In fact, your extremely advanced chefs will sometimes serve as many as *three* kinds of food, although I do not recommend that you attempt this yourself.

TO PREPARE: Follow the recipe for Food Heated Up, except use *two* food units, *two* pots, *two* stoves, etc. The trick is to select foods that "complement" each other, as illustrated by the following chart:

Okay. We've covered the two biggest potential problem areas involved in living together, namely dirt and food. This leaves sex, which in the interest of decency we will put in a separate chapter.

TYPE OF FOOD	COMPLEMENTS	DOES NOT COMPLEMENT
Meat	Ketchup, beer	Meat
Foods from cans (beets, ravioli, etc.)	Foods from bags, beer	Cool Whip (usually)
Other	Beer	Jerky°

°Consult with physician

CHAPTER 3

A Frank, Mature, Sensitive, and Caring Discussion of Human Sexuality with Dirty Pictures

NOTE: THE MATERIAL PRESENTED IN THIS CHAPTER WAS REVIEWED AND APPROVED BY THE OMAHA BOARD OF CENSORS. PICTURED ABOVE ARE MEMBERS: THE REVEREND FATHER JAMES J. FITZGERALD, CHAIRMAN; MRS. ELSIE MOYER; CAPT. ELROY FENTON, OMAHA P.D.; ESTHER BLATT; AND VERNON EPP.

Special Advance Warning to Decent People

I'm afraid that, in this chapter, we must talk about sex in a very explicit manner, because we want to expand the Frontiers of Human Understanding and also we want to sell as many books as possible to adolescent boys. This means we are going to have to use certain highly

21

clinical sexual terms, such as "puberty" and "mollusk," which can lead to arousal in some instances. So if you have a shred of decency in you, you'll want to stop reading and go make fudge or something until this chapter is over. You'd better leave right now, because the heavy pornography starts almost immediately after these asterisks.

          *   *   *

Still with us, eh? Ha Ha! Don't feel ashamed. You'd be surprised at some of the readers we get in this chapter.

Okay. Now that we've cleared out the religious fanatics, let's take a look (so to speak) at . . .

The Major Male Sexual Organs

The major male sexual organs are the testaments, the nomads, the doubloons, the inner tubules, the vasal constrictors, the reversion unit, and of course the Main Organ, or "wiener."

Men are very protective of these organs. This is because Mother Nature decided, apparently as a prank, to place them on the *outside* of the male body, where they are most likely to get hit by baseballs, or punched by small children,

or even—this makes me cringe, just thinking about it—attacked by crazed birds. And what is worse, Mother Nature made these organs extremely sensitive.

You know how women are always talking about the Pain of Childbirth, and how awful it is, and how men will never really understand it? Well, we men don't wish to make a big deal about this, but if you women really want to experience *pain*, you ought to try being male and taking a line drive to the privates. Yes sir. When this happens in a professional baseball game, and the player is down on the ground, writhing in agony, obviously clutching his private parts, the color commentator always says to the announcer: "Looks like he had the wind knocked out of him, Ted." But the male spectators know better, and if you look around you'll notice that they're all hunched over protectively, thousands of them, as if a sudden epidemic of Bad Posture Disease has swept through the crowd.

What this means is that, as they are growing up, males develop an attitude about their sexual organs very similar to the one that overprotective, doting parents have about their children. This is not a problem when the organs are young and innocent and basically dormant. But things change drastically when we reach puberty.

"IT'S A LINE DRIVE UP THE MIDDLE !"

Puberty generally occurs in males about two years late. By this I mean it occurs about two years after it occurs in females, which is somewhere around sixth grade. I remember at the end of my fifth-grade year, when we left for summer vacation, and the boys and girls were all just about even in the race for adulthood. But when we got back the next fall, the girls suddenly, out of the clear blue sky, were all a foot taller and had somehow acquired bosoms and God only

FEMALES USUALLY EXPERIENCE THE
ONSET OF PUBERTY BY THE SIXTH GRADE

MALES USUALLY EXPERIENCE THE ONSET
OF PUBERTY BY THE EIGHTH GRADE

knew what else. It was as though they had all attended Summer Bosom Camp.

This gives the girls an unfair head start. They get two whole years in which to get used to having sexually advanced bodily parts, and the result is they develop a certain maturity about it, a coolness of judgment, a savoir faire, that they retain for the rest of their lives.

Boys, meanwhile, are condemned to two years of wandering around the corridors of the junior high school, their eyes cruelly positioned by Mother Nature at just about bosom level, and consequently they develop this tremendous

yearning to catch up. When puberty finally strikes them, this pent-up desire has become so powerful that they develop erections that last for an average of slightly over three years. You men out there know what I'm talking about. The main reason adolescent males carry school books is they need something to hold in front of them.

Okay, then. To summarize what we have, in the typical healthy young male: We have a creature who tends to be highly indulgent toward his sexual organs, and we have organs that are semi-out-of-control much of the time, and almost always Ready to Party. Now let us contrast this with the sexual development of the typical female, starting with a discreet and sensitive examination of . . .

The Major Female Sexual Organs

I don't know what the major female sexual organs are. I get extremely confused just looking at the diagrams. Frankly, I don't think *anyone* really has a handle on the entire female reproductive system, because the organs are located inside the female body, where you can't see them. The only way a woman can

have even a vague idea of what's going on in there is to have a gynecologist root around with primitive implements, and perhaps even call in an associate for consultation ("Hey Bob! Come in here! What do you make of *this?!*").

So in contrast to men, who are always touching themselves and giving themselves little nicknames, women develop an attitude of almost clinical detachment about their reproductive systems.

Furthermore, where men's organs seem to be carefree and impulsive, women's are serious and hard-working, with a single-minded devotion to the idea of having a baby. No matter what the woman is doing on the outside—having a

THE SEXUAL ORGANS ARE EASY TO LOCATE ON THE HUMAN BODY. TRACE A LINE WITH YOUR FINGER FROM YOUR NAVEL TO YOUR KNEES. SOMEWHERE ALONG THIS LINE YOU WILL FEEL SOMETHING. IF YOU FEEL A BUMP, CHANCES ARE YOU'RE A MALE. IF YOU FEEL A DIP, THEN YOU'RE PROBABLY A FEMALE. IF YOU FEEL BOTH A BUMP AND A DIP, THEN YOU'RE A LITTLE BIT OF BOTH BUT NOT ENOUGH OF EITHER.

STEP 1: LOCATE YOUR NAVEL

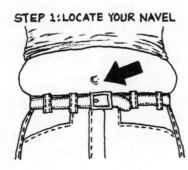

STEP 2: TRACE TO YOUR KNEES

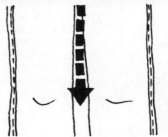

career, writing a novel, bowling—her organs are busy on the inside, gathering food for the baby, fixing up the baby's room, etc. At the end of each month they sigh, throw everything away and start all over again, thus sending the woman the friendly biological reminder: "Okay. Fine. Go ahead and have your fun out there. Don't mind us in here, slaving away, trying to ensure the very survival of the human race."

In summary, then, we see that, because of the location and nature of their respective organs, women tend to have a more serious, thoughtful, and responsible attitude toward relationships than men do. I realize this is an absurd generalization, but my feeling is that if

we can't have absurd generalizations, we might as well not even bother to write books.

Answers to Common Sexual Questions

Q. How long should sexual intercourse last?

A. This is an area of some disagreement between the sexes. As a rule, women would like to devote as much time to foreplay and the sex act as men would like to devote to foreplay, the sex act, and building a garage. This tends to lead to dissatisfaction on the part of the woman, who is often just beginning to feel pleasantly sensuous when the man is off rooting around in the refrigerator to see if there's any Jell-O left.

Q. Well, isn't there some sensitive and caring and loving technique that a couple can use to slow the man down?

A. Yes. When the woman senses that the man is nearing climax, she can whisper: "The Internal Revenue Service called again today, but don't worry, I hung up on them."

Q. I am a good-looking woman, as you can see from the enclosed glossy color photographs of me naked.

A. Yes. Thank you.

Q. Although I have an otherwise wonderful marriage, my husband seems to be losing interest in me sexually. It's the little things: he hardly ever smiles at me; he often works late; and he comes home with as many as four naked women. So I thought, to rekindle the old flame, I'd surprise him, using a method suggested by Marabel Morgan in her book *The Total Woman*, namely greeting him at the door wearing only Saran Wrap. However, we were out of Saran Wrap, so I used Tupperware, which I feel is a better product anyway, but this unfortunately failed to produce the desired result, in the sense that when my husband saw me, he suffered some kind of seizure, and I had to drive him to the hospital while attempting to cover my private parts with two quart canisters and a Deviled Egg Transporter. My question is: Can we deduct this mileage on our income tax?

A. That depends on your individual situation.

Q. Listen, I, ummm, I have this kind of weird sexual hangup, which is that I, ummmm . . . this is *very* embarrassing . . .

A. Go ahead! Say it! Don't be ashamed! That's what we're here for! To help!

Q. Okay, but I want to whisper it. (whisper whisper whisper)

A. My God! Really?

Q. Um, yes.

A. The Joint Chiefs of Staff?!

Q. Well, yes.

A. How do you get the hamsters into the accordion?

Necking Tips for Guys

The big problem with necking is figuring out whether or not your date wants to Do It. On the Planet of the Ideal Women, your date would just come right out and tell you. She'd say: "What do you say we lie down on the couch and neck like crazy?" Or: "Although I like you as a friend, I frankly would not neck with you even if the alternative were death by leeches."

But here on the planet Earth, she won't say anything. Sometimes this means she isn't interested. But sometimes it doesn't. Generally the way a guy finds out specifically what his date is thinking is at some point he lunges at her, lips puckered, and she responds by either puckering back, or quickly turning her head sideways, in which case the guy winds up sort of licking her hair, looking like a world-class dork. There is no face-saving way for a guy to get out of this situation, other than to have an instantaneously fatal seizure.

Assuming your date is responsive, your next move is to attempt "French-kissing," which is when you stick your tongue into her mouth, and she sticks her tongue into your mouth, and so there the two of you are, with your tongues in each other's mouths. This is a really sexy thing to do, according to French people, although you should bear in mind that they also like to eat snails.

HOW TO FRENCH-KISS

STEP 1: OPEN YOUR MOUTH AND STICK OUT YOUR TONGUE

STEP 2: STICK YOUR TONGUE IN YOUR FRIEND'S MOUTH, AND THEY STICK THEIR TONGUE IN YOUR MOUTH.

STEP 3: DON'T FORGET ABOUT THOSE HANDS!

STEP 4: GET IN THE CAR, WAVE GOODBYE TO THE PARENTS, AND GO OUT ON YOUR DATE!

Anyway, assuming your date seems to be responding positively to you, in the sense that she has not yet kneed you in the groin, and also assuming that you really and truly respect her as a human being and love her and plan to marry her, it's time to move on to . . .

Heavy Petting

The big problem here is the bra strap. You cannot casually unhook a bra strap. The bra-strap industry sees to this. Scientists over at the Bra Strap Research Center in Amarillo, Texas, work night and day with volunteer males and lifelike female dummies (see illustration) coming up with newer and more complicated fastening devices, devices where the first hook actually re-hooks itself after you go on to the second one, such that nobody can get these bras off, especially not a lust-crazed male in a dark room. Many priceless jewelry collections are now protected solely by bra straps.

If you get through the bra strap, your next challenge is the undergarments, which you will probably have to ask your date for assistance with, because they can be complex beyond human imagining, but I strongly advise that before the two of you tackle them, you should leave the restaurant.

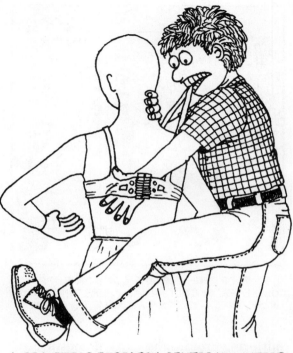

A BRA-STRAP RESEARCH CENTER VOLUNTEER TACKLES THE LATEST DESIGN

Solid Advice about Condoms

Guys, you should definitely use a condom. All major health authorities agree on this. The whole nation has become violently pro-condom, not just for guys having sex, but also for guys

95% OF THE WORLD'S CONDOM SUPPLY COMES FROM COLOMBIA, WHERE THE CONDOM BUSH, *CITCALYHPORP REBBUR*, IS GROWN

mean—the cover always is a picture of a handsome and of course brooding man embracing a woman with green eyes and a bosom that is clearly heaving, sometimes most of the way out of her dress. The title is always something fairly humid, like *Loins of Passion*.

You sexually inexperienced couples should get hold of one of these books, because inside you will find a number of passages that are chock-full of explicit, down-to-earth, practical "straight talk" about the sexual act:

"As Sabrina gazed upward at Baron LeGume, whose dark, brooding

puttering around the yard, domestic animals, most vegetables, and all major war monuments. Better safe than sorry!

Where to Get Additional Explicit Helpful Information on Sex

The best source of reliable information is romance novels, which you can find in better bookstores and supermarkets everywhere. You know the books I

DIAGRAM OF A TYPICAL ROMANCE NOVEL COVER

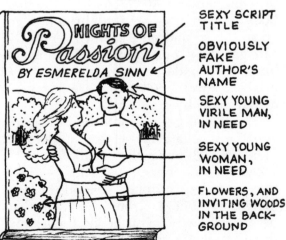

SEXY SCRIPT TITLE

OBVIOUSLY FAKE AUTHOR'S NAME

SEXY YOUNG VIRILE MAN, IN NEED

SEXY YOUNG WOMAN, IN NEED

FLOWERS, AND INVITING WOODS IN THE BACKGROUND

eyeballs were turgid with passion, she felt the tormented tenseness of his throbbing, pulsating malehood, and she knew, with a knowledge borne of knowing, that she could no longer hold back the surging waves of passion that washed over her, like waves of something, as his brooding throbbing pulsating highly engorged lips sought hers, not that she wanted to hold them back, we're talking about the waves of passion here, although she knew that somehow, somewhere, perhaps deep within the shuddering throes of year-ninghood that even now gripped the very core of her womanhood, if you get what we mean, that she must find a way, through the hazy mists of desire, to end this sentence, although she sensed somehow that . . ."

And so on. You young couples should study these helpful and realistic passages thoroughly, so you can use them for guidance when you are attempting sex ("You mean to tell me *that's* the tormented tenseness of your malehood?").

CHAPTER 4

Breaking Up or Getting Engaged

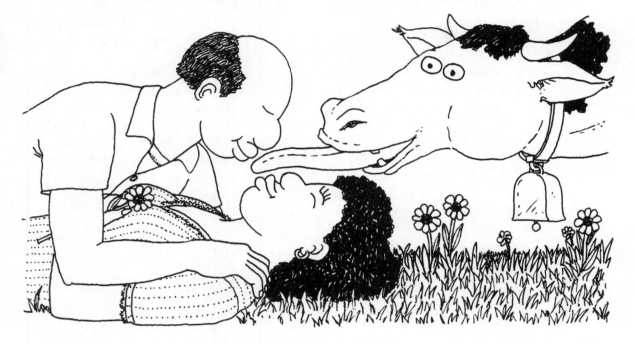

After a while, the sparkle tends to go out of a relationship. I don't care how passionate you are. I don't care if you're like those couples in romantic movies who, in the scene where they finally realize they're in love, lunge into each other's arms and fall to the ground, wherever they are, even if it is a pasture, and roll around amongst the cow doots in a sexual frenzy. You don't think those couples keep that kind of thing up, do you? Throughout life? Of course not. What would their clothes smell like?

The point being, a relationship can survive on pure romance for only so long. Sooner or later, Mundane Reality starts to seep in, and you need to make a decision:

• Do you break up with this person and look around for another one in hopes of once again experiencing the searing surge of unbridled passion, ideally in a carpeted environment? Or,

- Do you accept that your relationship can move to a more-mature stage, a stage based not so much upon impulse and romance and physical attraction as upon liking the same television shows? In short, do you get married?

How to Tell
If You Are Compatible
with Somebody

One way to find out if another person is "right" for you is to spend a lot of time with this person, talking and sharing experiences, so that you really get to know him or her as a human being. This is what we call the old-fashioned, or "stupid" way. The modern way is to take a Compatibility Quiz.

The Compatibility Quiz is a concept that was developed by top research scientists at *Cosmopolitan* magazine, a highly informative publication whose cover always has a picture of a glamorous woman, wearing an extremely low-cut outfit, whose breasts appear to be pointing straight up. In fact, they are pointing

down: Cosmopolitan suspends these women by their feet from the ceiling. That is the price you have to pay, if you truly wish to be glamorous.

Anyway, if you want to know whether your relationship will work out, you need to sit down and answer these questions:

Money

Who do you feel should be the "breadwinner" in a family?

A. The man.
B. The woman.
C. H. Ross Perot.

Children

Which of the following statements best describes your feelings toward children?

A. "Put that down this instant!"
B. "I said *put that down!*"
C. "*Never* put your finger in that part of the doggy!!"

Housework

In a modern marriage, who do you feel should be responsible for the housework?

A. Nobody.
B. Leona Helmsley.
C. It should be divided up fairly and equally among the servants.

Recreation

Your idea of a pleasant romantic evening is:
- A. Sipping a glass of wine and watching a roaring fire.
- B. Drinking a few martinis and roaring at the fire.
- C. Drinking a bottle of gin and setting things on fire.

Sex

The kind of sex you enjoy most is:
- A. With another person.
- B. With several other persons, but no animals.
- C. At least not invertebrates.
- D. Unless they are fairly tame.

Religion

How would you describe your attitude toward religion?
- A. About your height, only thinner.
- B. I am not especially big on religion, but I have watched it on television.
- C. I am religious to the point of human sacrifice.

Family Crises

Bill and Denise are a young married working couple with no children. One day they set out from Reno, Nevada, on foot at exactly 4:30 P.M. Bill walks three miles per hour and rests for ten minutes each hour, while Denise walks at exactly two miles per hour without stopping. After a couple of days they are both dead from scorpions. Which of the following statements most closely matches your feelings regarding this?
- A. It serves them right.
- B. I hear Reno is quite nice.
- C. I myself prefer a moister climate.

Current Events

The capital of Vermont is:
- A. Where they keep the governor.
- B. Very cold.
- C. Probably in New England.

HOW TO SCORE: Give yourself one point for each answer. No, what the heck, give yourself *two* points for each answer. Now add up your points and compare your total with the total for the person you're trying to be compatible with. If both of your totals are numbers, odds are you two will hit it off pretty well. At least until you get married. Or maybe not. How the hell should I know?

Your total:	Your potential mate's total:

Alternative Method for Stupid People

Another excellent way to decide whether another person is compatible with you is to use astrology. The word "astrology" comes from the Greek or possibly Latin words "astro" and "ology," so right away we can see that it is very scientific. In fact, astrology rests on a proven principle, namely that if you know the exact positions where the moon and the various planets were when a person was born, you can get this person to give you money. The way you do this is by making up random, semi-unintelligible pieces of advice, such as "attend to future considerations."

To use astrology for your own personal benefit, simply locate your astrological "sign" on the following chart, then look up your horoscope in any

YOUR BIRTHDAY		YOUR ASTROLOGICAL SIGN
Jan. 15–Feb. 13		VIRGIL
Feb. 14–Mar. 18		AQUARIUM
Mar. 19		NEPTUNE
July 20–July 3		LEON
Labor Day		PSORIASIS
June 6 at around 2:30		BOB L. HOCKMUNSTER, JR.
Giants° 6–Dodgers 3		SNEEZY

°Clinched playoff berth

reputable newspaper and govern your entire life accordingly:

Most people believe that breaking up is easier than working at a relationship. Hahahahaha.

How to Break Up

The ideal way to break up is the one featured in the famous best-selling book, *Love Story*, where the beautiful heroine, sensing that the relationship is getting maybe a little stale, contracts a fatal disease. In real life, however, it's never that easy. You never have a really good excuse for breaking up with the other person, so you feel guilty, and you put off confronting the problem. I have a friend who found it so difficult to tell his girlfriend he no longer loved her that he just kept going along with the program, until finally, one day, they actually got married. They had a big wedding, and she was up there, in front of all her friends and family, thinking this was the happiest day of her life, and he was standing there in a rental tuxedo, thinking: "Should I tell her now? Nah. Better wait till after we cut the cake." This kind of thing happens all the time.

So if you're going to break up, you have to overcome your guilt and break up *now*. Otherwise you'll never find the person you really want, the person with whom you can achieve your goal of Lifelong Happiness. You should follow the example of famous former ravishing beauty Elizabeth Taylor, who sheds husbands like used Kleenex and has consequently achieved Lifelong Happiness dozens of times.

Of course your major concern, in breaking up, is how to do it in such a way that the other person doesn't get so upset that he or she stabs himself or herself. Or yourself. I recommend that you take the honest approach. Come right out with the truth. That is always best, in the end. To build up your courage, practice holding imaginary conversations with your lover, wherein you set forth, calmly and rationally, the reasons why you feel the breakup is necessary, then try to imagine, and sensitively respond to, the various objections your lover might have:

YOU: Listen, I, um, I, uhh . . .

YOUR LOVER: Yes? Is there something you wish to tell me?

YOU: Um.

YOUR LOVER: Are you trying to tell me that, although you care for me deeply, and you will cherish always the times that we have had together, you

FOUR POPULAR METHODS OF BREAKING UP
USE "RENT-A-BOYFRIEND" SERVICES
I'M SORRY NORMAN, BUT I CAN'T GO OUT WITH YOU ANYMORE. MY NEW BOYFRIEND HERE, BRUNO, WILL EXPLAIN EVERYTHING TO YOU, IF YOU WISH...
YO, NORM!
USE YOUR TELEPHONE ANSWERING MACHINE
HELLO! THIS IS TOM SPEAKING. I'M NOT HOME RIGHT NOW, SO PLEASE LEAVE A MESSAGE—UNLESS THIS IS DOROTHY CALLING ME, IN WHICH CASE YOU CAN GO JUMP IN A LAKE! I NEVER WANT TO SEE YOUR FACE AGAIN! YOU'RE DULL... YOU'RE COLD... GET LOST!
BEEP!
USE A GORILLA MESSAGE SERVICE
DEAR GLEN, GET LOST! JULIE
LEAVE A NOTE ON YOUR FRONT DOOR
DEAR CAMILLE, I HATE TO TELL YOU THIS, BUT I'M DEAD. THAT MEANS I WON'T BE ABLE TO GO OUT WITH YOU ANYMORE. I HOPE YOU REALLY UNDERSTAND? SORRY, SPIKE

really feel that we both need more space to grow and enrich our lives as separate individuals? For my sake as well as yours?

YOU: Well.

YOUR LOVER: Then perhaps it would be best if we broke up, with no hard feelings or remorse on either side.

YOU: Okay by me.

After you've mentally rehearsed this dialogue enough times, you simply go through it again, out loud, but this time in the presence of your lover. You'll be surprised at how smoothly it goes:

YOU: Listen, I, um, I, uhh . . .

YOUR LOVER: If you break up with me, I'm going to kill myself.

YOU: I was thinking we should get married.

There! See how easy that was? I am so very happy for the both of you! Onward to our "Important Prenuptial Chapter."

CHAPTER 5

Important Prenuptial Chapter

Should you and your spouse-to-be have a prenuptial agreement? We put this question to five of the country's leading attorneys, and they sent us bills totalling $63,500. This should give you an idea of how important it is to try to avoid those pesky legal squabbles that could crop up down the road. So just in case, we have prepared the following Low-Cost But Fair Prenuptial Agreement for you. Of course, as is the case with any binding legal document, we strongly suggest that, before you sign it, you place it on a flat surface.

Low-Cost but Fair Prenuptial Agreement

BE IT HEREBY AGREED that since (*name of bride*), hereinafter referred to as The Bride, and (*name of groom*), hereinafter known as The Groom, have decided that they love each other with a deep and undying passion, at least for the time being, and consequently want to get married,

THEREFORE they do hereby agree that, in case later on for some reason God forbid they decide to get a divorce, they will both adhere to the following Deal:

1. MONEY. If there is any money, it shall be divided up equally and fairly between The Bride's and The Groom's attorneys.

2. DISHES. The Bride and The Groom shall equally divide up such dishes as have not been reduced to microscopic shards in the Traditional Pre-Divorce Violent Shrieking Kitchen Argument.

3. WEDDING-GIFT FONDUE SETS STILL IN THE ORIGINAL UNOPENED BOXES. The Bride and The Groom shall each keep eight fondue sets, and the rest shall be given to charity.

4. OTHER POSSESSIONS. The Bride shall get to keep whatever she picked out, including the living room, dining room, and bedroom furniture as well as any major appliances, carpets, lamps, paintings, etc. The Groom shall get to keep the Rolling Stones album *Get Yer Ya Yas Out* and the NHL Power Play table hockey game, including both pucks.

5. FRIENDS. Friends shall be divided up by sex and distributed accordingly.

6. RELATIVES. The Bride and The Groom shall each keep whatever relatives they had at the time of the original marriage. If there is any question about this, such as Uncle Bob, whom nobody can remember which family he belongs to, then he shall be allowed to visit either The Bride or The Groom, at his discretion, with the provision that he leaves after a couple of weeks.

7. DOG. The dog shall be the property of whichever party was supportive of it and cleaned up after it the time it was throwing up what looked like raccoon parts on the bed.

Tips for the New Bride

HOW TO GET ALONG WITH YOUR MOTHER-IN-LAW: Your best bet is drugs.

DEALING WITH YOUR HUSBAND'S OLD BUDDIES: Odds are your

IT'S NOT EASY TO CHOOSE BETWEEN YOUR WIFE AND YOUR BUDDIES!

husband will have old buddies from college or reform school with whom he has shared many important Male Bonding Experiences such as fighting and burping and taking turns driving cars into the lobbies of major hotels.

After you are married, you should not try to cut him off from these friends. They are a very important part of his life. They are able to discuss with him, as you cannot, a lot of important questions that guys are concerned about, such as: Who was pitching for the Yankees when Bill Mazeroski hit the bottom-of-the-ninth home run that won the 1960 World Series for the Pirates? Now you are continuing to read this paragraph, but believe me, your husband stopped at the end of the last sentence and is now staring at the ceiling and saying: "Whitey Ford? Nah.

Louis Arroyo? Nah." This is why he needs his buddies. To resolve questions like this.°

So you should make a special effort to make your husband's buddies feel welcome in your home. Invite them over for dinner. Invite them on your honeymoon. Don't make a big scene if they leave beer cans in the aquarium. And above all, don't force your husband to choose between them and you. I am not suggesting here that your husband would leave the woman he has pledged to spend the rest of his life with just so he could hang around with a bunch of guys talking sports and drinking beer. I am saying they would probably also order some pizza.

°It was Ralph Terry.

CHAPTER 6

How to Have a Perfect Wedding No Matter What

I am going to assume, in this chapter, that you're getting married for the first time and consequently you want to do it in the most traditional and ludicrously elaborate way possible. Those of you who are getting married for the second or third time will probably want a low-key, informal wedding. I know this was the case when my wife and I married

each other. It was the second wedding for both of us, and the most formal and organized part of it (I am being serious here) came when the wedding party played Capture the Flag.

Similarly, some friends of mine named Hannah and Paddy had their second-time-around wedding in a bar, amidst a dense haze of cigarette smoke and much loud drinking, such that the actual ceremony, performed by a judge, was barely noticeable. The judge kept trying to get people's attention by pounding on the bar and shouting, "Quiet down! We have to marry Hannah and Paddy!"

But first-time marriers usually prefer to have a traditional wedding, defined by experts as "a wedding where the flowers alone cost more than Versailles." One advantage of this kind of wedding is that, over the years, the various responsibilities have clearly been divided up between the bride's family and the groom's family:

RESPONSIBILITIES OF THE BRIDE'S FAMILY: The announcement; the church; the invitations; the clergyman; the rehearsal; the bridesmaids' luncheon; the flowers; the dresses; the reception; the food; the liquor; the photographer; the limousines; lodging and transportation for out-of-town guests; gratuities; the honeymoon; the national defense; a nice thoughtful present for the newlyweds such as a house.

RESPONSIBILITIES OF THE GROOM'S FAMILY: Not throwing up on the other guests.

Of course there is one other major responsibility of the groom, which is to buy the engagement ring. Guys, I know it can be intimidating to walk into a jewelry store and try to handle a slick salesman, but you'll do fine if you know a few basic technical facts about diamonds.

Diamond Formation

Millions of years ago, lumps of carbon fell down on the ground and got covered up by dirt and mountains, after which they were subjected to intense pressure by lobbying groups such as the National Rifle Association. Over the years, these lumps were buried deeper and deeper beneath the Earth's surface, so that today we don't even know where the hell they are. Nor care.

Meanwhile, shopping centers began to form, and inevitably they developed jewelry stores. This is where we stand today.

How Diamonds Are Measured

The standard unit of measurement for diamonds is called the "carat," which basically measures how much you love your fiancee. A guy who is only

A LARGE STONE CARRIES A LOT OF WEIGHT

mildly attracted to his fiancee will buy her a ring with only a few carats, whereas a guy who really loves his fiancee will buy her a stone so large that she can never again swim in ponds for fear she will become embedded up to her shoulder in bottom muck.

That takes care of the groom's responsibilities; everything else is up to you brides-to-be. You're going to be very, very busy planning your wedding, because naturally you want everything to be perfect. Remember at all times, brides-to-be, *this is your own very special day, and it damned well better be*

perfect or you are going to kill yourself with a cyanide capsule, which it is the responsibility of the maid or matron of honor to provide.

Actually, planning a wedding is not all that difficult, provided you do almost nothing else for the better part of a year. Naturally, this will be a very busy and exciting time for you. But as you go through it, you must make sure, amid all the excitement and hustle and bustle, that you don't lose sight of the whole point of the wedding—its deeper meaning and the central reason for its entire existence. Your gown.

Your Wedding Gown

Listen up, brides. You get only one shot in your life at a real wedding gown, and you better not blow it. Because a wedding gown is more than just a dress. It's a dress that costs a whole ton of money. It's a dress that you'll cherish for several decades in a box in a remote closet, perhaps to be taken out one day by your daughter when she's looking for (sniff) a wedding gown of her own. She'll wisely reject yours, of course, because by that time it will have served as the home environment for 60,000 generations of insects. The last thing she wants, when she's up at the altar on her

A WEDDING DRESS SHOULD NOT BE THAT "SOMETHING OLD"

own Very Special Day, is for a millipede to come strolling out of her bodice.

Nevertheless you must have a wonderful gown. This is where you need the expert help of a qualified bridal couturier, who can answer your technical questions:

YOU: What kinds of gowns do you have for under $2,000?

COUTURIER: Well, we have this one right here.

YOU: This is a group of used Handi-Wipes sewn together.

COUTURIER: Yes. By preschool children.

With this kind of guidance, you'll be able to select a truly memorable gown, one that will cause your parents to remark in admiration: *"How much?! That's more than we spent on our first house!"* If they don't make this remark, your gown is not memorable enough, and you should take it right back to the couturier to have some more pearls glued on.

After you've selected your gown, it's time to get on with planning the rest of the wedding. This task will be easier if you use this convenient Wedding Planner Checklist:

Bride's Wedding Planner Checklist
Six Months before the Wedding

This is the time to choose your wedding site. It should be extremely traditional. Ideally, you want St. Paul's

Cathedral, in London, England. This is where Princess Diana got married to Prince Charles in a ceremony that lasted longer than a number of major wars. Also it required more horses. This is the kind of memorable wedding you definitely want to shoot for.

If St. Paul's is not available, look for a large traditional religious building, such as a church or synagogue, closer to home. In many cases, these buildings are affiliated with major religions, which may require that you hold specific religious beliefs before you can get married there. This is a good thing to check out beforehand, by calling up the person in charge:

YOU: Hi. I was thinking of getting married in your church or synagogue, and I was wondering if I had to hold any specific religious views.
RELIGIOUS PERSON: Why yes, you do.
YOU: How many?
RELIGIOUS PERSON: Let's see, here . . . five, six . . . looks like eight in all.
YOU: Fine, fine. Could you please mail me a set?

If the building is really right for you, with adequate parking and every-thing, you should go ahead and agree to hold the beliefs, even if they involve animal sacrifice. This is your wedding, after all.

The other major things that must be accomplished six months before the wedding are:
- The bride should select a caterer and a nice country club for the reception, and her parents should withdraw their life's savings so they can put down a deposit.
- The mother of the bride and the mother of the groom, if they do not already know each other, should have a luncheon wherein they get along about as well as Iran gets along with Iraq.

Five Months before the Wedding

Now is the time to select your bridesmaids. This is a very large honor, which you bestow only upon people who meet the following criteria:

1. They should be female.
2. They should be willing to wear bridesmaids' dresses.

This second criterion is the most important, because the whole point of the bridesmaid's dress is to render the person wearing it so profoundly unat-tractive that she cannot possibly outshine you, the bride. In fact, one of the really fun things a bride gets to do is go to the bridal salon with her mother, and the two of them get drunk and howl with laughter as they consider various comical outfits that they might encase the bridesmaids in. Some of them go so far as to select actual clown suits, but most prefer the traditional look, which is:

 • Long frilly dresses in bright pastel colors reminiscent of Bazooka bubble gum or some experimental and ultimately unsuccessful ice cream flavor with a name like "Pumpkin Surprise."

 • "Puffed" sleeves that make any woman who is larger than Audrey Hepburn look like a Green Bay Packer.

 • Large "fun" floppy hats that obscure the bridemaid's face so thoroughly that you could use men if you really had to.

You need not feel restricted to this look, however. This is your Very Special Day, and you can make the bridesmaids

ALTERNATE BRIDESMAIDS' OUTFITS

FOR UGLY PEOPLE'S WEDDINGS   FOR BIKERS' WEDDINGS   FOR APPALACHIAN WEDDINGS

wear anything you want. Veils, fur stoles, whalebone corsets, hats with waxed fruit, kneepads, anything. Remember: they have to pay for it.

Four Months before the Wedding

This is a good time to select a silver pattern and a groom. (see Chapter 1, "How to Find Somebody to Go on Dates With"). In fact, your smart modern bride will often select several grooms, so as to guarantee that in case one or two of them get "cold feet," she'll still be able to have her Very Special Day.

You must be much more careful in selecting your silver pattern. It should have a name similar to the ones developers give to shoddy new apartment complexes, such as "Coventry Downe Manor"; and each place setting should consist of a regular fork, a dinner fork, a breakfast fork, a snack fork, a soup fork, a holiday fork, an emergency fork, a Care Bear fork, a Pez dispenser, and the equivalent knives, spoons, ladles, scone handlers, beet prongs, tuffet churners, prawn smelters, and clam goaders. Remember: Your silver is your first major family heirloom, to be cherished and stored in the same closet where you cherish your wedding dress until such time as one of you files for divorce.

Three Months before the Wedding

This is the time for the formal announcement of your engagement to appear in your local newspaper. Your local newspaper should have a name like *The Morning, Afternoon & Evening Chronic Spokesperson-Fabricator,* and the wording of the announcement should be as follows:

"(*Your parents' names*) are extremely relieved to announce the engagement of (*your name*) to (*your fiance's name*), who is not really good enough, son of (*your fiance's parents' names*), who are quite frankly dreadful, but (*your parents' names*) will settle for just about anything at this point because suitors are not exactly knocking down (*your name*)'s door despite all the money (*your parents' names*) spent on her teeth. An elaborate wedding is planned."

This is also when you send out your invitations. You are naturally going to want to invite me and a number of my friends, because we are a lot of fun at any kind of affair where there is free liquor, plus if the band is really lame, which it will be (see page 50), we are not afraid to express our displeasure by hurling segments of the prime rib entree, which by the way may be served buffet-style for informal afternoon weddings. Others you might consider inviting include your family and any member of the groom's family who can produce a receipt proving he or she has purchased at least one full place setting.

The wedding invitation should be worded as follows:

The invitation should be on a little card, which you mail to your invitees along with a little matching R.S.V.P. card and a return envelope that says POSTAL SERVICE WILL NOT DELIVER WITHOUT STAMP.

Mr. and Mrs. Bob A. Doomus
Request the Honour and the Favour
of You Showing Up at the Marriage of
Their Daughtour

Salina Fennel
to
Mr. Dwayne R. LePoon, Jr.
or
Mr. Bill V. "Scooter" Fencemender
Depending On If Dwayne Can Get Off Work

at Our Lady of Recurring Lower Back Pain Religious Church
Saturday, the Twenty-fifth of June
at 1:30 o'clock P.M. Fahrenheit
Bring a Gift

R.S.V.P.   No tank tops

We Already Got a Fondue Set

Two Months before the Wedding

This is when the mother of the groom should go out and buy a dress to wear to the wedding that is fancy enough so that the mother of the bride will be convinced that the groom's mother is trying to upstage the bride, and consequently the bride's mother will think about virtually nothing else for the rest of her life.

This is also when you should hire a band. It makes no difference which one. All wedding bands are the same. They're all cloned from living cells that were taken from the original wedding band, "Victor Esplanade and his Sounds of Compunction," and preserved in a saline solution in Secaucus, New Jersey (which, incidentally, is also the home of the first native American Formica trees). They'll show up in stained tuxedos, and no matter what kind of music you ask them to play, they'll play it in such a way that it sounds like "New York, New

VICTOR ESPLANADE AND HIS SOUNDS OF COMPUNCTION

York." Really. If you feel like dancing to some rock 'n' roll, and you ask them if they maybe know "Honky Tonk Woman," they'll say, "Oh sure, we know that one," and they'll play "New York, New York." They can't help it. We're talking genetics.

One Month before the Wedding

Now is the time for you and the groom to get your blood tests. If your groom's blood fails, get another groom. If your blood fails, get some new blood. We are much too far into the planning process to turn back now.

By now you should also have lined up a photographer. You'll want to have lots of photographs of your wedding to show to your family and friends, who will have been unable to see the actual ceremony because the photographer was always in the way.

Often you can save money by having your pictures taken by a friend or relative who is familiar with photography in the sense of owning a camera and knowing where a Fotomat is. I have some good friends named Rob and Helene who took this approach, and the pictures came out really swell except that for some technical reason there is no light in any of them. Just these vaguely human-oid shapes. We all love to get these pictures out and look at them. "Look!" we say. "There's Helene! Or Rob! Or the cake!"

Two Weeks before the Wedding

By now your advance wedding gifts should have started to arrive, including at least 14 attractive and functional fondue sets. Also by this time the bride should start to notice a scratchy feeling at the back of her throat, indicating that she is just starting to come down with a case of Mongolian Death Flu.

One Week before the Wedding

This is where the groom starts to get actively involved in the wedding preparations, by having a "bachelor's party" where he gets together with his "chums" for one last "fling" and wakes up several days later in an unexplored region of New Zealand. Meanwhile you, the bride, are bustling about, looking after the hundreds of last-minute details, having the time of your life despite the intermittent paralysis in your right leg.

The highlight of this week, of course, is the Rehearsal Dinner, when the wedding principals, especially the immediate families, take time out from the hectic pace of preparations to share in an

A TYPICAL BACHELOR'S PARTY

evening of warmth and conviviality, cul-
minating when the mother of the bride
and the mother of the groom go after
each other with dessert forks.

The Wedding Day

This is it! The biggest day of your
life, and there's no way that any dumb
old 108-degree fever is going to put a
damper on it!

A good idea is to put your wedding gown on early, so the sweat stains
can expand from your armpit areas and
cover the entire gown, and thus be less
noticeable. And now it's on to the wedding site!

As the guests arrive, the ushers
(What do you mean, you forgot the ushers?! Get some!!) should ask the guests
whether they want smoking or non-

smoking, and seat them accordingly (except the mother of the bride and the mother of the groom, who should be seated in separate states). Then, at the appointed time, the organist should start playing a traditional song, such as "Here Comes the Bride" or "Happy Birthday to You," and the wedding procession should come down the aisle, in the following order:

1. A cute little nephew, who will carry the ring and announce, at the most dramatic part of the ceremony, that he has to make poopy. If you have no cute little nephew, rent one.

2. The groom (if available).

3. The bridesmaids, walking sideways to minimize the risk that they will injure a member of the audience in the eye with their puffed shoulders.

4. You, the bride, the Center of Everything, smiling radiantly, your eyes sparkling like the most beautiful stars in the sky until, as you reach the altar, they swell shut in reaction to the antibiotics.

From that point on, it will all be a happy blur to you—the ceremony, the reception, dancing with your new husband to your Special Song ("New York, New York"). Enjoy it all, for you'll never have a wedding like this again, even if you do recover fully.

IT'S ALL SMILES FOR THE PHOTO SESSION!

THE TRADITIONAL "CUTTING OF THE CAKE"

THE MODERN "CUTTING OF THE CAKE"

(WHO GETS TO SLICE THE FIRST PIECE SHOULD BE DECIDED IN ADVANCE)

But the best part of all will come later, on your Wedding Night, just the two of you, alone at last—you in your filmy, lacy, highly provocative peignoir, and your groom on his back in the shower snoring and dribbling saliva on his rental tuxedo. My advice to you is: relax, have a glass of wine, and check his pulse every 15 minutes. Don't be alarmed if he has none. This is normal, for grooms.

Pranks

It is the responsibility of the best man and the ushers to play fun and comical pranks on the Happy Couple, such as—this is a good one!—just before they come rushing out of the reception, ready to leave on their honeymoon, you take their car and—get this, guys!—you sell it and keep the money. Ha ha! The Happy Couple will sure talk about *that* for a number of years!

The Honeymoon

Most couples prefer to take their honeymoons away from the familiar and the ordinary, to go to an exotic, different, and foreign place, such as Epcot Center. I am not kidding here. A lot of couples really do honeymoon at Disney World. Of course they don't admit this. They say they're "honeymooning in Florida," because they don't want people to know that the highlight of the whole wild lustful romantic adventure was shaking hands with Goofy.

Of course there are plenty of other possibilities for your honeymoon. Your friendly travel agent will give you

THE NEWLYWEDS HAVING A WONDERFUL HONEYMOON

mounds of brochures from all kinds of resorts desperate to obtain your honeymoon dollar:

For A Honeymoon Memory That Will Long Remain Lodged in the Esophagus of Your Mind...

Sea Cucumber Island

"Your Personal Little Wad of Paradise"

Nestled in the aromatic waters of the Houston Ship Channel, situated within easy traveling distance of such popular attractions as Houston, Texas; Interstate 10; and Paris, France,* Sea Cucumber Island offers everything you need to make your "dream honeymoon" become extremely real:

• A complimentary glass of Manischewitz Extra Dense Cream de Grape Champagne Wine** upon your arrival to "toast" the happy couple.

• Fully flushing toilets*** in many rooms "Sanitized for Your Protection."

• Food.****

• Ping-Pong.*****

ENJOY SWIMMING IN OUR WARM, PLACID WATERS

ENJOY TOURS OF THE BAY OF CUCUMBERS

PRICES START AS LOW AS $299******

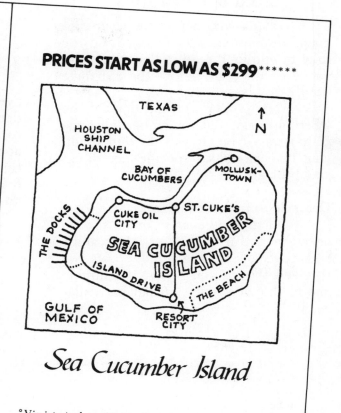

Sea Cucumber Island

*Via jet airplane. Not included.

**We get to drink it.

***In some cases.

****If the Vend-o-Matic man came. Not included.

*****You supply paddles and balls. And table. Also net.

******Does not include anything.

Thank-You Notes

Thank-you notes are your last major responsibility as a bride, and the rules of etiquette require that you try to get them all done before the marriage legally dissolves.

The proper wording depends on whether or not you remember what the people gave you. If you do remember, your note should say specific nice things about the gift:

Dear Mr. and Mrs. Sternum:

Thank you ever so much for the very thoughtful fondue set. Mark and I feel that, of all the fondue sets we received, the one you gave us is definitely one of the nicer ones, in that particular color.

Sincerely,
Elaine and Mark

If you don't remember what gift they gave you, you'll have to compensate by sounding very grateful for it:

Dear Mr. and Mrs. Sternum:

We just don't know how we can ever thank you for the extremely wonderful gift you gave us. It has become the focal point of our entire lives! We think about it all the time. We are seriously thinking about quitting our jobs and forming a religious cult that just sits around all day worshipping this gift.

With Extreme Sincerity,
Elaine and Mark

CHAPTER 7

Newlywed Finances

HOUSEHOLD MONEY MANAGEMENT

It's sad but true that money causes a great many unnecessarily fatal squabbles among newlyweds. Very often this is because of a difference in priorities. For example, you want to buy food, while your spouse wants to buy a thoroughbred racehorse. It's important, in these situations, for both of you to be willing to sit down together and try to achieve a workable compromise. In this case, you could buy a thoroughbred racehorse and eat it.

Often, however, the solutions are not that simple. This is why it's so important that right now, while you're just starting out, you draw up a realistic household budget. I can help you here. I have lived in a realistic household for many years, and I would say, based on experience, that your typical weekly expenses should run pretty close to the following:

```
┌─────────────────────────────────────┐
│    REALISTIC WEEKLY HOUSEHOLD        │
│      BUDGET FOR TWO PEOPLE           │
├─────────────────────────────────────┤
│ Food that you buy and               │
│ eventually eat .............. $30.00 │
│                                      │
│ Food that you buy and store in      │
│ the back of the refrigerator until  │
│ you have to throw it out because    │
│ it looks like the thing that burst  │
│ out of that unfortunate man's       │
│ chest and started eating the        │
│ spaceship crew in the movie         │
│ Alien ........................ 55.00 │
│                                      │
│ Pennies that you get as change and  │
│ put in a jar, intending to someday  │
│ put them in those wrappers and      │
│ take them to the bank, when in      │
│ fact you will die well before you   │
│ ever get around to this ...... 117.48│
│                                      │
│ Rent, clothing, car payments,       │
│ insurance, gas, electricity,        │
│ telephone, magazines ......... 829.12│
│                                      │
│ Miscellaneous ............. 2,747.61 │
└─────────────────────────────────────┘
```

As you can see, there are a lot of expenses associated with running a household, and to meet them, you will need Financial Discipline. Each week, when you get your paychecks, you must set aside $3,779.21 right off the bat, to cover your weekly household budget. If your combined weekly paychecks total less than this amount, perhaps you should go back and marry a rich person (see Chapter 1). Your other option is . . .

Credit Cards

Credit cards are an excellent source of money. The way they work is, people you don't even know mail them to you, and then stores, for some reason, let you use them to actually *buy* things. (No, I can't figure it out either!)

The thing is, you have to be responsible about how you use your credit cards. You can't just rush out and charge every single item in the store. Think ahead! How would you fit it all into your car?

So I strongly recommend that you be cautious with credit, following the wise Borrowing Rule of Thumb employed by the federal government, which is: "Never borrow any amount of money larger than you can comfortably pronounce."

HOW TO MAKE YOUR OWN CREDIT CARD

STEP 1

CUT A 3⅜-INCH STRIP OFF OF A SHEET OF THIN WHITE PLASTIC.

STEP 2

CUT A 2⅛-INCH STRIP FROM THE 3⅜-INCH STRIP, CROSSWISE.

YOU SHOULD END UP WITH A 2⅛-BY-3⅜-INCH CARD.

STEP 3

USING A LAUNDRY MARKER, WRITE THE WORDS "MAJOR CREDIT CARD" ON ONE SIDE IN OFFICIAL-LOOKING LETTERS. ADD SOME STARS, WORDS, EAGLES, OR OTHER NEAT STUFF TO PERK THINGS UP.

MAJOR CREDIT CARD
BANK OF OMAHA

STEP 4

USING A FRIEND'S MAJOR CREDIT CARD, SANDWICH YOUR "MAJOR CREDIT CARD" AND YOUR FRIEND'S CARD TOGETHER ON A COOKIE TIN AND BAKE FOR 15 MINUTES AT 500 DEGREES.

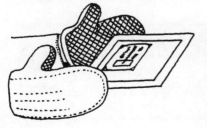

STEP 5

AFTER CARDS HAVE COOLED, PEEL THEM APART. YOUR CARD SHOULD HAVE YOUR FRIEND'S NAME AND NUMBER NEATLY INDENTED IN IT. THEN FILE THE CORNERS TO A ROUNDED APPEARANCE.

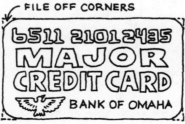

FILE OFF CORNERS

6511 2101 2435
MAJOR CREDIT CARD
BANK OF OMAHA

STEP 6

ON THE REVERSE SIDE OF THE CARD, POSITION A 5/16-INCH STRIP OF BLACK TAPE ABOVE A 5/16-INCH STRIP OF WHITE TAPE. SIGN YOUR FRIEND'S NAME. YOUR CARD IS NOW READY TO USE.

BLACK TAPE   WHITE TAPE

Elwin Feeg

Your Checking Account

This is another potential source of money, although it's usually impossible to tell how much money is in it. The important thing is to try to keep your checkbook "balanced." Here's how.

1. Each month the bank will send you an envelope containing a bunch of used checks, which, for tax purposes, you should place in a two-ply grocery bag and eventually misplace. Also in the envelope will be:

• A little note entitled "TO OUR CUSTOMERS!" that will feature a cheerful and totally unintelligible message like this: "Good News! First Fiduciary Commonwealth National Savings & Loan & Bank & Trust is now offering 3.439087654% Growth Bonds of Maturity yielding 2.694968382857% Compound Annualized Rate of Secretion!" You should try to save this note, for tax purposes.

• A piece of paper covered with numbers (your "statement").

2. Okay. Now open up your checkbook and take a look at the kind of checks you have. If you have the kind with little nature scenes printed on them, or, God help us, little "Ziggy" cartoons, you're much too stupid to balance your own checking account, and you should definitely go back and marry a rich person (see Chapter 1).

3. Now examine your check "register" (the part of your checkbook that you sometimes write on). It should look like this:

4. Now compare and see if any recognizable numbers on the "register" are the same as any numbers the bank has printed on the "statement." If you find any, you should put a little happy face next to them, like this: ☺

5. If your total number of happy faces is five or more, then your account is what professional accountants call "in balance," and you can go on ahead and watch TV. If you score lower than five, you should get on the phone immediately and explain to your bank that they have made some kind of error.

Your Home: Buying vs. Renting

Aside from Madonna and Sean Penn, most newlyweds rent their first home. This can actually be a pleasant experience, as you discover the Fun Side

THERE ARE STILL MANY INTERESTING HOUSES AVAILABLE FOR NEWLYWEDS

of apartment life: getting to know your new neighbors; listening to what kind of music your new neighbors like to play very early in the morning on their 150,000-watt sound system; having your new neighbors' legs come through your ceiling when water from their leaking toilet rots their floor, etc.

But sooner or later, despite this recurring joy of these communal experiences, you're going to want to have a place of your very own. Step one is to figure out how expensive a house you can afford. This depends on your combined annual incomes, as is shown by the following chart:

YOUR COMBINED ANNUAL INCOME	PRICE OF HOME YOU CAN AFFORD
Up to $20,000	Don't be an id-
$20,000–$40,000	iot. There are no
$40,000–$80,000	homes that you
$80,000–$100,000	can afford.

But don't despair, young couples! You can still realize the dream of owning a home of your own, provided you're willing to do what generations of newlyweds have done before you: roll up your sleeves, do the hard work, and make the tough sacrifices involved in nagging your parents for a down payment. They probably have some money left, even after your wedding, and your job is to whine and wheedle and look pathetic until they give it to you. Make sure you leave them something for food:

COST OF YOUR NEW HOME	AMOUNT YOUR PARENTS SHOULD HAVE LEFT FOR FOOD AFTER LENDING YOU THE DOWN PAYMENT
Up to $50,000	$150
$50,000–$100,000	$75
Over $100,000	Various canned goods.

CHAPTER 8

How to Argue Like a Veteran Married Couple

Most young couples begin married life knowing very little about how to argue with each other, and are forced to learn through trial and error. Sadly, some of them never do learn, a good example being that couple on "The Waltons" who never fought about anything, and consequently wound up with three or four hundred children.

There is no need for this kind of tragedy. We veteran married couples have, over the years, especially on long car trips, developed certain time-tested techniques that even an inexperienced person can use to turn any issue, no matter how minor, into the kind of vicious, drawn-out argument where you both spend a lot of time deliberately going through doors you don't really need to go through, just so you can slam them viciously.

When you get involved in marital arguing, the role model you want to bear in mind is World War I, which got started when some obscure nobleperson, Archduke Somebody, got assassinated way the hell over in the Balkans, and the next thing you know people in places as far away as Cheyenne, Wyoming, were rushing off to war. These were people who wouldn't have known a Balkan if they woke up in bed with one, but they were willing to get shot at because of what happened there. It's the same with a good marriage argument. If you really

ARCHDUKE SOMEBODY

do it right, you should reach the point where neither of you has the vaguest recollection what the original disagreement was, but both of you are willing to get divorced over it. This is the kind of veteran marital relationship you young couples can develop, if you follow these proven techniques.

The most important technique is: *Always be on the lookout for conversational openings that can lead to arguments!* To illustrate this, let's look at a typical marital conversation:

MARY: Honey, could you please try not to leave your socks on the coffee table?

JOHN: Why of course, dear. I'm sorry.

Pretty pathetic, right, married couples? Mary has created the perfect opening for a good argument, and John has *totally* dropped the ball, by admitting he was wrong. *Never admit you're wrong, young married persons!*

Now you're saying, "But what if John's socks are right there, on the coffee table? How can he argue about *that?*"

The answer is: He can't. So what he has to do is, he has to somehow get the argument, or at least his end of it, focused on a *completely different topic*, ideally a *strident accusation* that he has *dredged up out of his memory* and that is *totally unrelated to the issue at hand.* This is very important, young married persons: You must always maintain a supply of retaliative, irrelevant accusations in your mind, so that you can dredge them up when you need them.

Let's say, in this case, that John once thought Mary was flirting with her old flame Bill at a party. This is a good thing to accuse her of in the current argument, as it is totally unrelated to the coffee table. However, John must be careful how he brings it up; if he does it *too* abruptly, Mary could become confused, and the argument could end right there:

MARY: Honey, could you please try not to leave your socks on the coffee table?

JOHN: Oh *yeah?* Well what about your old flame, Bill?

MARY (confused): Huh?

So what John needs to do—this is the essential skill of marital arguing—is to come up with a smooth way to get from *Mary's* topic to *his* topic. This technique is called a "segue," (pronounced "segue"), and if you do it right, it will usually lead to a whole new series of mutant topics you can argue about. Let's see how it works:

MARY: Honey, could you please try not to leave your socks on the coffee table?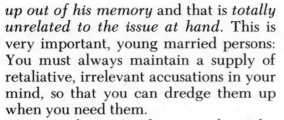

JOHN: Why do you always do that?

MARY: Always do what?

JOHN: Always look for things to criticize.

MARY: I *don't* always look for things to criticize. I just don't like finding your damn . . .

JOHN: Fine. Great. Curse at me. I didn't see you cursing at *Bill,* at the Johnsons' party.

MARY: What is *that* supposed to mean?

JOHN: Oh, come on. You were flirting with him.

MARY: I was flirting? And I suppose you weren't *all over* Jennifer?

JOHN: I don't see how you could have known what I was doing, after all you had to drink.

See how effectively this veteran married couple handled the situation? In just a few quick sentences, they have

CREATIVE ARGUING IS THE KEY TO
A LONG-LASTING MARRIAGE

gone from a seemingly unpromising top-ic, socks, to a whole treasure trove of issues that they can debate and dredge up again for years to come. I'm not saying you young couples will get this kind of results your first time out of the gate, but with a little practice, you'll get the hang of it, and it can lead to the discovery of a whole new facet of your relationship (see Chapter 11, "How to Put New Life into Your Marriage or Else Get a Divorce").

CHAPTER 9

Children: Big Mistake, or Bad Idea?

SMILE, KIDS!

FAMILY PORTRAIT

In this chapter, we're going to talk about how children affect your marriage. We're *not* going to talk about how you actually produce the children in the first place. We covered that topic thoroughly in an earlier book, *Babies and Other Hazards of Sex*, which explores the whole area of childbirth in great detail and reaches the following scientific breakthrough conclusions:

1. It is very painful.
(If you'd like additional facts on this topic, you can read the book, although it doesn't contain any.)

For now, however, we're going to talk about how your married life will change *after* you have children, so that you'll be able to carefully and rationally weigh the pros and cons of parenthood, then barge right ahead and have children without any understanding of what you're really getting into, just like everybody else.

What It Really Means to Be a Parent

What it really means to be a parent—note this carefully, because it's the essence of the whole thing—is: You will spend an enormous portion of your time lurking outside public-toilet stalls.

For reasons that modern medical science has been unable to explain, children almost never have to go to the bathroom when they are within eight or nine miles of their own home toilets. It does no good to try to make them. Tell a child to go to the bathroom before you leave home, and the child will insist that not only does he or she not have to go *now*, but he or she will probably never have to go to the bathroom *ever again.*

And of course when you get where you're going, let's say a restaurant, the child will wait until your entrees are about to emerge from the kitchen, then announce that he or she has to go. Children are incredibly sensitive to approaching entrees.

So you will take the child to the bathroom, and, if it is an especially loath-

some bathroom, a bathroom that has clearly not been cleaned since the fall of Rome, a bathroom where the floor is littered with the skeletons of Board of Health employees who died attempting to inspect it, if it is *this* kind of bathroom, the child will immediately announce that he or she has to do Number Two.

And of course you must stay there with the child. The child will want you to stand *right outside* the toilet stall, while the child goes in there, and ... and nobody really knows. It's a real mystery, what young children do in public-toilet stalls. Whatever it is, it takes them longer than it took you, the parents, to produce them in the first place.

What I hate about this is that restaurant men's rooms are often fairly small and intimate places, and while I'm standing there, waiting for my son, strangers are constantly coming in to pee, and there I am, inches away from them, lurking there with no apparent purpose, like some kind of sex pervert who *likes* being in disgusting men's rooms. So, to show that this is not the case, I try to keep a conversation going with my son. Except the only thing I can think of to talk to him about is how the old Number Two is going. I mean, you'd feel like an idiot in that situation, talking about the Strategic Defense Initiative. So we have these ludicrous exchanges:

ME (brightly): So! Robert! How's it going in there?!

ROBERT (irritated): You just *asked* me that.

ME (grinning like a madman at the peeing stranger so as to reassure him that everything is okay): Ha ha!

Eventually, the child will emerge from the stall, when he or she is abso-

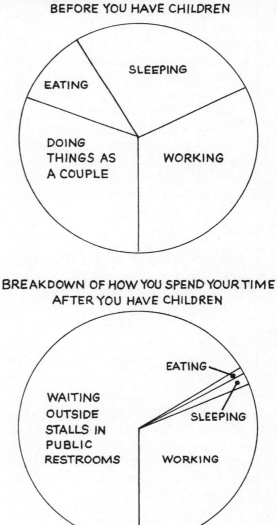

BREAKDOWN OF HOW YOU SPEND YOUR TIME BEFORE YOU HAVE CHILDREN

SLEEPING
EATING
DOING THINGS AS A COUPLE
WORKING

BREAKDOWN OF HOW YOU SPEND YOUR TIME AFTER YOU HAVE CHILDREN

WAITING OUTSIDE STALLS IN PUBLIC RESTROOMS
EATING
SLEEPING
WORKING

lutely sure that the entrees are stone frozen cold. The child doesn't care about the food, because children don't go to restaurants to eat. They go to restaurants to go to the bathroom and play loud shrieking games under the table, so that you, the parents, are constantly ducking your heads under and hissing, *"Stop that!"* like some deranged species of duck. The child never actually touches the food, which is why many modern restaurants are saving money by serving reusable children's entrees made entirely out of plastic.

Where Can I Find Decent, Affordable Child Care?

Hahahahahaha.

Forgive me for laughing in a bitter and cynical fashion, but you happen to have hit upon the most serious problem facing the Free World today: the international child-care crisis.

In the old days, of course, the Free World had an excellent system of high-quality, low-cost child care in this country, namely your mother. Unfortunately, however, your mother is no longer interested in caring for children. She is interested in spending what little is left of her life among furniture that does not have Hawaiian Punch stains all over it. And you, of course, can't engage in child care, because you need to get out and have a Rewarding Career so you can have a chance to earn enough money to pay for child care.

Except there is hardly any available. You go around checking out preschool facilities, and you keep finding yourself in dank basements where the staff is missing a large percentage of its teeth and the educational materials consist of four crayons—all burnt sienna— and a GI Joe doll with most of the limbs pulled off. The result is that people are desperate. People who work in New Jersey are dropping their children off each morning at child-care centers in Utah.

Fortunately there is some hope. A new company recently opened for business, called the Exactly What You Are Looking For Child Care Company. It has spacious, clean, modern, well-equipped facilities within walking distance of your home or office; it's open from 5 A.M. until as late as you want; and it's staffed by middle-aged British women who love children and attend church regularly and are all licensed pediatricians. The cost is $3.50 per child per day. If you're interested in enrolling your child in this excellent program, all you have to do is kill the Wicked Witch of the West.

BE SURE TO SELECT A CHILD-CARE CENTER STAFFED BY PEOPLE WHO ENJOY PLAYING WITH KIDS

How Children Affect Your Sex Life

Children are Nature's very own form of birth control. To illustrate how they perform this vital function, let's take a look at a minute-by-minute schedule, showing how my wife and I put our six-year-old son, Robert, to bed on a typical evening. To make sure we have some time to ourselves, we try to have him in bed by 8 P.M., which means we start the procedure a full hour earlier:

7 P.M.—We announce to Robert that it's time to get ready for bed.

7:04, 7:09, 7:12, 7:14, 7:17, 7:18, 7:22, 7:24, 7:25, 7:26 & 7:27—We announce to Robert that he really has to start getting ready for bed Right Now and we are Not Kidding.

7:28—Robert goes to his room and actually starts getting ready for bed.

7:29—Robert notices that his rubber Godzilla doll is missing. *How* he notices this, in a room containing roughly 78,500 toys, nobody can explain, but he does notice it, and of course all other activities must cease until we can resolve this matter because God forbid that a child should be required to go to bed without his rubber Godzilla doll.

7:43—We locate Godzilla and Robert begins getting ready for bed again. He is supposed to take off his clothes and put on his pajamas. He can do this All By Himself.

9:27—So far, All By Himself, Robert has removed his shirt and, if he is really on a roll, one of his shoes. I go in to help him along.

9:30—Now in his pajamas, Robert has his teeth brushed, which is the signal for him to announce that he is hungry. We tell him that this is his own fault, because he did not finish supper, and he absolutely cannot have any more food, no sir, forget it, not a chance, it's time he learned his lesson, etc.

9:57—Robert finishes a bowl of Zoo-Roni and submits to having teeth brushed again.

10:02—We read a bedtime story, *Horton Hatches the Egg,* by Dr. Seuss, which takes us quite a while because we must study every page very, very carefully in case there is some tiny detail we might have possibly missed when we read it on each of the previous 267 consecutive nights.

10:43—We announce that it's time to go to bed.

10:45, 10:47, 10:51, 10:54, 10:56 & 10:59—We announce that it really is time to go to bed Right Now and we are Not Kidding.

11:03—Robert actually gets into his bed. We tuck him in, kiss him good night, and creep silently out of the room, alone at last.

11:17—Robert falls asleep and is immediately awakened by a terrible nightmare caused by being in bed with his face six inches from a rubber Godzilla doll. We remove it.

11:28—We kiss Robert good night and creep silently out of the room, alone at last.

11:32—Hearing noise from Robert's room, we return to find him sobbing loudly. So upset that he is barely able to choke out the words, he explains that he has just realized that the mother bird in *Horton Hatches the Egg* loses her baby in the end, and even though she was terribly mean, she is probably very sorry by now, and very lonely. We try to explain that this is not at *all* the point that Dr. Seuss was trying to make, but Robert is inconsolable. Finally we agree to let him climb into bed with us, but "just for one minute."

2:47 A.M.—We return Robert to bed, kiss him good night, and creep silently from the room, alone at last.

3:14, 3:58, 4:26, 5:11 & 5:43—The household goes on Red Alert status as various routine nightmares occur, each one causing us to stagger, half-asleep, down the hallway, like actors in a scene from *Night of the Living Dead Parents.*

6:12—Dawn breaks.

Whenever I read newspaper stories about people who have, say, nine children, I never ask myself: "How do they manage to take care of them all?" I ask myself: "Where did they find the time to *conceive* them all?"

I don't mean to suggest, by what I've said in this chapter, that children are bad for a relationship. Because in the end, the negative aspects of being a parent—the loss of intimacy, the expense, the total lack of free time, the incredible burden of responsibility, the constant nagging fear of having done the wrong thing, etc.—are more than outweighed by the positive aspects, such as never again lacking for primitive drawings to attach to your refrigerator with magnets.

KIDS SURE CAN MAKE PESTS OF THEMSELVES

CHAPTER 10

How to Have an Affair

My first piece of advice is that if you're planning to have an affair, you should read this chapter in a safe place, such as the linen closet. You don't want to be sitting around the living room, in plain view of your spouse, reading a chapter entitled, in great big letters, "How to Have an Affair." I recommend that you hide this book under your garments and

say to your spouse: "Well, I guess I'll go sit in the linen closet with a flashlight for a while!" Your spouse will never suspect a thing. Unless you don't have a linen closet. That would be a dead giveaway.

Another dead giveaway is acting guilty. Let's take a typical person—we'll call him "Ed"*—who is having an affair with a woman at his office. If Ed has a

* Although his name is actually "Steve."

guilty conscience, he may accidentally reveal this in casual conversation with his wife:

ED'S WIFE: Would you like another corn muffin, dear?

ED: I'm having an affair with a woman in my office!

Even if Ed's wife is not a trained psychologist, she might conceivably gather, from certain subtle verbal "clues" Ed is subconsciously dropping, that something "fishy" is going on. Ed must make more of an effort to watch his words:

ED'S WIFE: Would you like another corn muffin, dear?

ED: I'm *not* having an affair with a woman in my office!

Most affairs occur at the office, of course, which leads us to another important rule of affair-having: *Never be discreet at the office.* To illustrate why this is important, let's consider two people, Ellen and Chuck, who have worked together in a large corporate office for several years, and have recently started having an affair.

Up to this point, Ellen and Chuck have probably been behaving the way men and women always behave in offices, which is to say: constantly winking and leering and engaging in loud and fun suggestive sexual banter. Behaving like lust-crazed fools has been a major form of entertainment in offices for as long as anybody can remember; in terms of total American corporation employee hours consumed, suggestive banter ranks well ahead of work, and only slightly behind making Xerox copies of personal documents.

But like so many couples, Chuck and Ellen, now that they are engaging in *real,* as opposed to pretend, sexual activity, suddenly decide they have to be discreet. They never banter. They never eat lunch together any more. They walk past each other without even looking at each other. When they are forced, by circumstances, to be together, they display the same kind of warmth and closeness toward each other as the Vice-president of the United States displays toward deceased heads of state. They are formal and cool.

They are also morons. The other employees, who, if they have been in the corporate world more than six weeks, have already witnessed hundreds of other major office affairs, will immediately recognize the cause of this sudden change in behavior. Ellen and Chuck might just as well go around wearing convention-style nametags that say:

HI! MY NAME IS
Ellen
I'M HAVING AN
AFFAIR WITH CHUCK!

Within days everybody in the office will know what's going on. The affair will be discussed extensively in staff meetings. It could well appear in the annual report to the stockholders.

What this means, of course, is that if you want your affair to go unnoticed by your co-workers, you have to be blatantly obvious about it. Chuck should wait until the office is extremely quiet, then stand up at his desk and shout across 47 desks to Ellen: "HEY ELLEN! WHAT DO YOU SAY WE MEET AT THE OUT O' TOWN MOTOR LODGE AFTER WORK TODAY AND HAVE SEXUAL INTERCOURSE!" And Ellen should shout back: "HECK YES!! I HAVE MY DIAPHRAGM RIGHT HERE IN MY PURSE!"

Chuck's and Ellen's co-workers would never suspect a thing. "What a couple of kidders Chuck and Ellen are!" the co-workers would chuckle.

How You Can Tell If Your Spouse Is Having an Affair

You can always tell. No matter how careful your spouse is, he or she is going to make a mistake somewhere, and you'll catch it, if you know the Major Warning Signs, which are:

1. Your spouse acts strange.

2. Your spouse, trying to trick you, acts normal.

If you notice either of these Warning Signs, you should wait until your spouse is in a vulnerable position, such as reclining in a dental chair, and then you should point-blank ask the following gently probing question (if your spouse is male): "*Well?* Who is she?"

Now listen closely to the answer. If it's something specific like: "You mean the person I'm having an affair with? She is Dorina Mae Swiggins," that means your suspicions are probably justified. But if it's something evasive like: "What are you talking about?" or "Who is *Who?*", then you quite frankly have to ask yourself how come your spouse is refusing to answer a simple direct question. Either way, this would be a good time to read the next chapter.

HOW TO TELL IF YOUR HUSBAND IS HAVING AN AFFAIR...

1. HE HAS SHIFTY EYES — IF YOU CAN SEE THEM!

2. HE STARTS LOSING SOCKS OR UNDERWEAR.

3. HE BRINGS HIS GIRLFRIEND HOME FOR THE WEEKEND.

HOW TO TELL IF YOUR WIFE IS HAVING AN AFFAIR...

1. SHE WEARS TURTLENECK PULLOVERS TO HIDE THE HICKIES ON HER NECK.

2. SHE TELLS YOU THAT HER NEW FISHNET STOCKINGS ARE FOR A LADIES CLUB PLAY.

3. SHE ACCIDENTALLY LOSES HER WEDDING RING SATURDAY NIGHT — JUST BEFORE GOING TO THE LADIES CLUB PLAY.

CHAPTER 11

How to Put New Life into Your Marriage
or Else Get a Divorce

Time takes its toll on every marriage. The sense of romance and adventure that you feel as you take your wedding vows on that bright Saturday afternoon in June inevitably gives way to familiarity and even boredom, often as early as 8:30 that evening. Yet some couples seem to go on happily forever, a

good example being Ferdinand and Imelda Marcos, former owners of the Philippines. Long ago, they discovered a secret that has worked its magic for many successful couples: thoughtfulness. Ferdinand and Imelda were always showing each other, in little ways, that they cared. For example, when Imelda would get depressed because of the hassle and strain of everyday life, plus the fact that she was bloating up like an inflatable life raft, Ferdinand would say to her: "Buttercup, you look depressed. Why not take the national treasury and purchase every luxury consumer object in France?" This thoughtful gesture never failed to perk her up.

Of course you may not be in a position to demonstrate quite that level of care, but there are things you can do to show your commitment to each other—little, thoughtful, romantic gestures that say you still think the other person is "somebody special." For example, you can:

1. Try to remember (you guys, especially) to flush the toilet.

2. Remember your spouse's birthday. "Hey!" you can say. "Wasn't your birthday last month?"

3. Go dancing, or even . . .

4. Go dancing with your spouse.

5. On your anniversary, give your spouse an appropriate traditional gift for whatever year it is, as shown on the accompanying chart:

A NIGHT OF DANCING WITH YOUR SPOUSE CAN BRING YOU CLOSER, OR AT LEAST ALLOW YOU TO RUB BELLIES FOR A WHILE

NUMBER OF ANNIVERSARY	TRADITIONAL GIFT
1st....................	Ore
5th....................	McNuggets
10th...................	Veg-o-Matic
15th...................	Oil change
20th...................	"Slim" Whitman album
30th...................	TV tray or assault rifle
40th...................	Frankincense
50th...................	Ointment
60th...................	Suppository
70th...................	Indonesian Fighting Snake

DR. EVA C. TUBBY PERFORMS DAVE'S SECOND WEDDING

6. Consider renewing your wedding vows. The best place to do this is Las Vegas, where "wedding chapels" are a major industry, along with divorce, gambling, and scorpion paperweights. My wife and I renewed our vows in Vegas a little while back, on a Friday the 13th, in the very same chapel (everything I am telling you here is the truth) where Joan Collins got married her third or fourth time. The whole thing took less than four minutes and cost only $50, plus a tip for the minister, who was named (I swear) Dr. Eva C. Tubby.

7. Go on a Getaway Vacation Fling. Just the two of you. One day, when the pressure gets to be too much, you should just say to your spouse, out of the

WHY NOT SNEAK OFF TO FLORIDA FOR A WEEK ?

blue: "Let's go!" Then you should impulsively throw a few items into a suitcase, jump into a cab, race to the airport, and hop on the next plane to Hawaii, or the Caribbean, or Europe, or wherever you want to go. Why not?

You'll be glad you did it. Once you're up in the air, settled back in your seats, sipping champagne (Why not?), the two of you can hold hands, close your eyes, and just let your minds drift away to . . .

THE CHILDREN!! MY GOD, YOU FORGOT THE CHILDREN!!! TURN THE PLANE BACK RIGHT NOW!!!

Sometimes, however, even thoughtful and romantic gestures such as these don't do the trick. Sometimes you find that the two of you, no matter how much you may once have cared for each other, are starting to drift apart. It's the little things that give you away: you hardly ever talk any more; you no longer kiss each other when you come home; you live in different states; etc. Maybe it's time to face up to the fact that you're just not right for each other any more. Hey, it happens. People change. They get older, they get larger, and sometimes they start to smell bad. Maybe the time has come to think about—let's come right out and say it:

Divorce

The most important thing is to get yourself a lawyer. Oh, I realize you probably think you and your spouse can work this thing out amicably without any third parties. But what if suddenly your *spouse* gets a lawyer, and you end up stone broke on the street wearing only a Hefty trash bag? You can't afford to take this chance. You need a lawyer, too, so you and your spouse can *both* end up wearing Hefty trash bags. I recommend the ones with the patented "Cinch Sak" drawstring top.

How to Select a Lawyer

The best way to select a lawyer is to watch late-night television, which is where your top legal minds advertise. You're looking for one who can demonstrate:

• *Integrity,* in the form of wearing a dark suit;

• *A sound knowledge of the law,* in the form of standing in front of a shelf with a lot of books on it; and

• *A sincere personal interest in you,* in the form of making the following speech: "Hello. I'm Leonard Packmonger, of Leonard Packmonger Legal Attorneys of the Law Associates. Does

your back hurt sometimes? Do you ever use consumer products? If so, I would say that, based upon my many, many weeks of experience in handling cases just like yours, you definitely have good grounds for a major lawsuit. Come on in and let's talk about it and sign some binding documents. Just for stopping by, we'll give you a free, no-obligation neck brace."

Grounds for Divorce

At one time it was difficult to get out of a marriage unless there was some kind of very serious problem with it, such as that one or more of the people involved had become deceased.

Today, fortunately, it is easier to get divorced in most states than to get a transmission repaired properly. The only requirement is that you have a legal reason, which is technically known as "grounds." If you have no grounds of your own, you can probably get some from your lawyer, who will have an ample supply left over from previous cases; or you can select some from this convenient list of grounds, all of which are 100 percent legally valid in every state in the union. Or at least they should be.

- Wearing shorts and black knee socks at the same time.
- Calling you "Sweetie Bean-cakes" in front of strangers.
- Forgetting to buy beer.
- Repeatedly putting the ice-cube tray back in the refrigerator with two or fewer ice cubes in it.
- Bringing the car home with just enough gas in it so that, if you shut the engine off and coast on the downhill slopes, you can get as far as the end of the driveway.
- Any cigar-related activity.
- Standing next to you with a sour facial expression at a party while you tell a really terrific joke and then loudly announcing the punchline three-tenths of a second before you get to it and then saying: "Isn't that AWFUL?" (NOTE: In some states this is grounds not only for divorce, but also for murder.)

- Golf.
- One day, with no warning, bringing home:
  1. a cat, or
  2. an Amway representative.
- Leaving his or her toenails in a prominent location as though they were decorative art objects.
- Using the word "frankly" a lot and not meaning it as a joke.
- Operating a loud household appliance during the Super Bowl.
- Secretly liking Geraldo Rivera.

The Divorce Proceedings

You want to keep them as quiet as possible. You don't want them to be highly publicized, like the divorce a few years back in Palm Beach, Florida, involving wealthy socialites Peter and Roxanne Pulitzer, in which Peter claimed that Roxanne had slept with a three-foot trumpet. Naturally the national news media found this to be far more interesting than anything that has ever happened in the Middle East, so now *everybody* has heard about it. Roxanne Pulitzer could visit a remote and primitive Amazon jungle tribe, and the tribespeople would all gather around her and make trumpet sounds.

YOU SHOULD BE PREPARED FOR ANYTHING DURING YOUR DIVORCE PROCEEDING – EVEN THE TRUTH !

So you want to avoid letting your intimate secrets out. Not that I am suggesting for one second that you have ever slept with a trumpet. You are more the bassoon type.

Starting Over
after the Divorce

Eventually the divorce will become final, and you can start picking up the broken pieces of your life and selling them to pay off your legal bills. But also you must think about the future, and, yes, meeting someone new. You must not be afraid. Oh, sure, you got burned and you got hurt. But that is no reason to give up. You must not be afraid. You must show the same kind of gumption as the cowboy, who, if he gets thrown off a horse, climbs right back on, and if he gets thrown off again, climbs right back on again, and so on, until virtually all of his brain cells are dead.

Back to Chapter 1.

Index